Every Step of the WAY

Actions Speak Louder Than Words

by

Teresa Petkau

Every Step of the WAY

Copyright 2019 by Teresa Petkau

Published by
Hidden Treasures Art Studio
19-33361Wren Crescent
Abbotsford, BC
Canada V2S 5V9
email: hidden.treasures.aitkenstudio@gmail.com

Cover Photo: Moira Connelly
Cover design: Jennifer Aitken & Teresa Petkau
Butterfly photo: Joyce Grubb

Story Editing: Michael Kerry
Book Formatting: Heartbeat Productions Inc. Win Wachsmann
Devotional: Sarah Young – Jesus Calling

Hope Nuggets: Teresa Petkau

Songs: Bert Petkau

ISBN: **9798609375469**

DEDICATION

This story is dedicated:

To the one I will always love my Saviour Jesus Christ.

To my precious Mom, Mary Bridget Muscat now in heaven with Bert.

To my special friends Jacqueline Luxon, Lisa Lowndes & Joyce Grubb. I cherish our woman-to-woman friendships. Thank you for faithfully staying the course with me.

To Glenith Ansley for all your prayers and the Christ-like beauty you display.

To my friends and family who have encouraged me and come alongside me as I continue to walk faithfully on my journey in life.

FOREWORD

In the spring of 2017, an attractive woman timidly introduced herself to me at a Lance Wallnau meeting in Lake Tahoe. Teresa and I learned we lived within an hour's drive of each other in British Columbia and exchanged contact information.

That brief connection has since developed into a meaningful and loving friendship.

During our early visits, Teresa shared her journey; the loss of her husband and best friend, Bert, lovingly written about in her first book "*A Fountain of Hope*" and the family's healing process as they learned to navigate life without him.

And then…Teresa started making plans.

Her intimate relationship with Jesus has been her firm foundation, her strength…first through heartache and then through the steep learning curve of meeting new challenges as her plans and dreams began to take shape.

This woman is gutsy! This woman perseveres! This woman overcomes! And remains humble and servant-minded, love in action.

A seasoned prayer warrior, you can be assured that God inclines His ear and honours her prayers.

Teresa's friendship is a pearl of great price. Be blessed as you read another hopeful story and journey of adventure.

Glenith Ansley

Friend & Intercessor

QUOTES

Start by doing what's necessary; then do what's possible, and suddenly you are doing the impossible.

Saint Francis of Assisi

www.brainyquote.com

Now faith is the substance of things hoped for, evidence of things not seen.

Hebrews 11:1 KJV

INTRODUCTION

Over the past thirty years or so, I have had the privilege to travel to many incredible countries in the world. Places that are uniquely different from one another and culturally nothing but distinctly their own. It is through these travels I have had the pleasure to meet so many different people and leave a mark of my own wherever my feet have trod. God has opened doors for me to encourage, pray, and deposit a measure of hope along the way through my ministry here on earth. My first book, *"A Fountain of Hope,"* has made its way to Europe, Australia, Scotland, Cyprus, and North America.

It is a true story about a love that ended too soon, and about a love that never ends. It is also a hopeful story about how well my family have grieved through the loss of a man we loved as a husband and a father. It tells how we grew through the journey and learned not to take anything for granted. We have brought hope to others who have experienced loss, as we all have in some way or another!

I am truly humbled and grateful for my experiences, because sometimes it is through tragedy that we find our silver linings. I have met people who have lost hope and struggled to understand loss, just as I have. God has provided strength for me in my life, and that has given me courage and an adventurous spirit to face some almost impossible situations and to overcome adversity.

This story is a new journey I have encountered, so come and enjoy another account of how I overcame the impossible, how I faced my fears head-on, and how I am learning to love as never before. If you love adventure and travel as much as I do, you will be inspired by this chronicle. I put one foot in front of the other to do what seemed beyond the bounds of possibility, and yet I was able to defeat every hindrance that came my way.

PURPOSE

The year 2018 was an unusual year for me. I lost some very special people in my life: my precious mother, my youngest sister's daughter, and some other friends who passed peacefully into eternity.

I have met others this year also who have experienced loss. Some of them feel discouraged and disappointed with life and question their ability to continue to hope! This story is intended to inspire hope and not only hope but a belief that love does change things. No matter what difficult circumstances come your way, when you choose to get up and carry on the path you are on, there is a strength that arises within your soul. It pushes you forward to live life fully and still have hopeful expectations. I had the audacity to keep going no matter what was happening through each one of my adventures in this story.

My mom would say to me, "Teresa life is a mystery to be lived, not a problem to be solved." I have pondered these words many times, and she was right. I have found that in the mystery of life each day, I know God is there, and nothing can bridle that courage He gives to each one of us.

I TELL MYSELF, "KEEP GOING; YOU CAN DO IT!"

Out of the depths of our beings is a desire to be loved, fulfilled, accepted, and to have purpose in this life. Each day presents us with a sequence of ongoing circumstances, and it is how we handle the situations that moves us forward or holds us back from entering into the very best that God has for each one of us. Through my own journey each day, I am finding that the most precious gift is living in God's peace. It gives me a relying confidence in Him that even through the unknown, He is there every step of the way to be by my side and to give me an ongoing hope through each moment of each day.

JESUS CALLING

Sarah Young

I AM THE POTTER; you are My clay. I designed you before the foundation of the world. I arrange the events of each day to form you into My preconceived pattern. My everlasting Love is at work in every event of your life. On some days, your will and Mine flow smoothly together. You tend to feel in control of your life when our wills are in harmony. On other days you feel as if you are swimming upstream, against the current of My purposes. When that happens, stop and seek My Face. The opposition you feel may be from Me, or it may be from the evil one.

Talk with Me about what you are experiencing.

Let My Spirit guide you through treacherous waters. As you move through the turbulent stream with Me, let circumstances mold you into the person I desire you to be. Say yes to your Potter as you go through this day.

* * *

These Scriptures remind you and me that He is the potter and we are the clay. I am so glad I can rest in the certainty that He knows what He is doing every day in all of the affairs of my life. Our part is to relax and trust in Him with faith.

Isaiah 64:8; Psalm 27:8

CULTIVATING LOVE THROUGH TRAVELS

In this narrative, I welcome you to my adventures of travel. Some of them are spectacular and endearing, some are risky and personal, yet in each one of them, there is reason to believe that through trusting God, nothing is impossible, even in the hardest physical or emotional tasks we face.

This includes trekking 300 km across Spain in September 2018 with two of my high school friends. Through the ups and downs of the hike, I met some amazing people and we shared stories with each other. That gave each one of us the courage and strength to finish our own personnel races. On this journey, I learned something new about love. I found an extravagant love, wrapped in grace, that changed my paradigm of how I view life and people.

Since then, I am finding, as I cultivate this love each day, my heart grows more with compassion for others. I am learning to be in the moment, to be aware of my surroundings and to bless someone that I meet each day with a kind word.

In my travels, I've had the privilege to meet people from far and wide across this planet, and many times, I gave away one of Bert's music CDs or simply shared God's love.

I welcome you to read about my ventures, and as you do, I trust this love will be evident throughout the pages. I hope you experience the wonderment of how God takes the broken pieces of our lives and makes a beautiful tapestry out of them as we make our way through the journey we all embrace each day. It's through the valleys we grow and not just by striving to get to the destination. It is in the trials that growth takes place, and wonderful memories are made. My friend Alfred Lee would say to me, Teresa from the ashes God makes diamonds out of our lives, and he sees you as a beautiful rare black diamond.

PILGRIMAGE OF HOPE

My recent and unexpected pilgrimage in Spain, along the Camino de Santiago, was shared with hundreds of fellow pilgrims. What a life-changing experience!

It showed me a God-given strength and courage and to overcome some difficulties along the way. I met many people, and each one of us shared a common thread, walking hundreds of miles across a land, each for our own particular purposes.

The word Camino from the Spanish translation to English means a path, a road, or a journey one takes. Aren't we all endeavouring to get through this planet on which we have been placed, hoping for something meaningful to take place in our lives?

Each one of us has a destiny to fulfill. It is a design unique to each one of our gifts and talents that have been placed in each one of our hearts. Are you wondering why you are here, perhaps searching for meaning in life, wondering do you really have gifts and talents? We all have aspirations deep within, and we should be tapping into the very core of who we are to recognize the talents and those gifts and to use them to bless and encourage others. Our aspirations are usually things we are good at or give us passion for life. They are rooted in love; which is what brings life to others. When we are alive to those things we love to do, we become whole and ready to have a desire to be free to bless others.

We can learn from the experiences we go through, and each one of us has a purposeful story to tell. My desire is to give hope to those who have experienced loss of some kind. I think we all can relate to loss in various ways. In each path we choose to walk, there is something to glean even through the storms we as individuals encounter along the way. No one's life is perfect - life is not a bed of roses, and neither is it a bed of thorns. It is a choice; a choice we make every day, how we affect the outcome of our future.

HISTORY OF CAMINO DE SANTIAGO

Those who walk this route, Camino De Santiago (the Way of Saint James), are called pilgrims, meaning travelers, on a special path or a holy journey to somewhere that represents something of significance. All of the participants walk their own personal passages, with some doing it in parts or sections, while others walk the whole 790 km trek into the town called Santiago de Compostela in northwestern Spain. To walk the whole pilgrimage takes about a month and a half.

The apostle James was one of the disciples who was present at the crucifixion and burial of Jesus Christ. After the resurrection of Jesus, James went about sharing the gospel throughout Spain. He returned to Judea and was eventually martyred for his faith in Jerusalem, and his body was sent back to Spain. The bones of Saint James, (Santiago) are said to be laid in the cathedral Santiago de Compostela in Galicia.

In the early days of the 8th-century, monks and others walked the path to commemorate their faith and to honour those who had passed on. As they walked this pilgrimage they reflected on such mysteries as: What is the meaning of life?

It is said that in the earliest of times, individuals would go down to the seashore to get a shell and when their journey was completed they would hand in a shell as a way of saying they had finished their pilgrimage upon arrival to the cathedral in Santiago de Compostela. Thousands and thousands of individuals have walked or biked the Camino over the years.

Today when you register, you are given a passport to get stamped each day either in a church, hotel, hostel, or café along the way. You are also given a scalloped shaped shell that represents, as in the days of old, that you are a pilgrim walking the Camino. The shell is hung on your backpack to be noticed as you meet and pass other pilgrims along the way.

This ancient pilgrimage starts in the Pyrenees mountains in the beautiful French town called Saint-Jean-Pied-de-Port. This is where you register and are given your passport and shell. Your name is put into a computer and if you decide to come back later to finish the walk you are listed in the registry. The passport, when stamped each day, gives evidence where you have walked and how many miles you have covered along the way. Those who complete the whole Camino walk

proceed into the cathedral to receive a
Certificate of completion.

Passport and shell

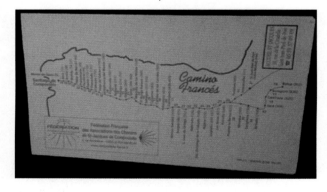

The Route

THE WAY

The Spanish Camino is my most recent accomplishment. It is a pilgrimage with a common theme that offers a quiet space to face situations, hurts, disappointments, and overcome the internal battles we face within ourselves. Each day of this venture as you walk reflecting and sorting through your thoughts in the stillness of the day, you learn a lot about yourself and what you are made of. The physical and emotional challenges of the walk may be difficult at times, yet the beauty of the surroundings is amazing. Trekking across a foreign land and embracing the unique Spanish culture as you enter each village makes way for the mystery, the unknown, and the risk of accomplishing something so rewarding.

On this globetrotting expedition, I met many different people from around the world, traveling like myself one day at a time. All of us considered ourselves to be pilgrims, and this made the walk one of the most eventful and fulfilling ventures I have pursued.

It was freeing to disconnect from the internet and the constant ringing of a cell phone. I remember listening to the clanging sound of my water bottle against my backpack strap in the silence as I walked up and down the many paths. As I took each step, I could hear the tinkling back and forth of the scalloped-shaped shell tied to the back of my pack. The shell was a symbol of identification that we were all walking the Camino. As we passed each other, we would politely say *"**Buen Camino**,"* meaning *"**Good Way**."* In other words, *"**Have a good journey!**"*

As you embark with me through many of the joys and challenges in this story, I hope you find your own Camino to bring you closer to finding true peace within. May you find adventures that will truly be rewarding, even giving you hope to walk out your own expeditions in the future.

As we walked for miles and miles each day, I heard the tapping of the walking sticks upon the ground, and I heard my breath increase when we were hiking up steep inclines. Often I would feel my heart pumping outrageously, and then I would remind myself that I could do this, even when my legs almost felt like they could not go on.

The rewards were there. Taking the time to be still and look around to enjoy the beauty of mountains in the distance, vineyards with rows and rows of luscious grapes, grassy meadows and even rugged ancient paths of rock hedges snaking across a landscape thousands of years old. We heard the sounds of trickling streams under ancient bridges as we hiked across an unfamiliar land, filling our water bottles at old stone fountains engraved with weathered Roman numerals.

We also climbed some very steep hills and overcame the scorching heat to reach our destination each day. These were some of the little victories we discovered.

What made this the best adventure, were the people I met from various countries around the world. The timing of our meetings was no accident, and some of their stories were funny, sad, endearing, and at times, even examples of divine intervention.

I will share many of them, and I will share how they impacted me with a quiet confidence and contagious hope to run my race without ever giving up.

I learned during some of these encounters what it means to love people right where they are. Through the ugliness and shame, they were experiencing, I tried to understand how a walk across Spain could bring healing and hope to their broken hearts.

I learned to color outside the lines of a perfect picture and to listen. I found that I could be still and even step out when I felt uncomfortable, and be courageous to speak truth when it was necessary.

Mostly along the way, I met brave individuals walking the Camino to prove to themselves that they could overcome something difficult in life. Some were there for the adventure of walking this famous route and some, like myself strove to accomplish walking 300 km across northern Spain. All of us would make memories of special days with like-minded pilgrims journeying together to simply walk one step at a time as we fulfilled a lifetime goal.

Backpack and Camino shell

Our feet the afternoon before day one

Trekking Shoes

My gear

A Camino Marker

CARRYING ON

It has been four years now since my husband Bert went home to heaven, and I have learned by the grace of Jesus Christ to navigate my life in a new way. My heart has healed slowly through the bruises and scars, never understanding the timing of tragedy, yet always looking for the silver lining in it all. Through the grief and heartache, I have taken each day to heal, to be courageous and to be brave, acquiring newness of life and learning to surrender much, love others with a deep compassion and to be grateful for the life God has given me.

Life is a journey unfolding each day, and I am learning from every experience that I embrace. No matter what has come my way, I am thankful for how things are falling in to place in my day-to-day affairs even when I don't always understand what it all means. I continue to walk out my destiny, and I realize God truly looks after those who trust Him. Every story has a lesson worth learning. As you read about my travels during the past four years, I hope you glean from some of my experiences how to get up when you are down. We must never give up on the strength and courage that lies within each one of our hearts and always have a measure of hope.

This story is special because it is an adventure. My two high-school friends and I were curious to see where it would take us. I have included in this endeavour other meaningful travel exploits of my life, hoping these experiences also will encourage readers to step out into their open doors, to reach horizons dreamed about and the impossible situations we face in life that sometimes seem unattainable. God is always waiting patiently for us to look up and to trust in His never-ending love, to realize that He does have a plan and a purpose a destiny to step into and that plan unfolds one day at a time and one step at a time.

Hope Nugget: Taking time to seek and believe nothing is impossible.

I BELIEVE IN MIRACLES

My life from the start has been one of many miracles, evident as I look back upon my past. My adventurous spirit was birthed when God had a plan for my life and knit me in my mother's womb. I was born in the later 1950's, the second oldest of eight children. At birth, I weighed only two pounds, and my twin sister weighed two pounds, six ounces. Life looked very different back then, without the conveniences we have today. In those days, mothers did not know they were expecting twins, and the modern technology wasn't available to take care of premature babies. We were both put into incubators for twelve weeks, and our parents had to trust that the right amount of oxygen would keep us alive; too much would cause us to go blind. I can't imagine what Mom and Dad went through, not being able to hold their two firstborn children. Now, as a mother myself, I know how difficult that would have been.

Years later I remember my mom telling me that when we were released from the hospital, she could fit me in a drawer and for awhile a dresser drawer in their bedroom became my crib for several months. I believe God from the very start had a plan for my life even though I did not realise that until my later teen years.

> Psalm 139:13-16 ESV
> *For you formed my inward parts; you knitted me together in my mother's womb. I praise you, for I am fearfully and wonderfully made. Wonderful are your works; my soul knows it very well. My frame was not hidden from you, when I was being made in secret, intricately woven in the depths of the earth, your eyes saw my unformed substance; in your book were written, every one of them, the days that were formed for me, when as yet there were none of them.*

How intimate and detailed is this Psalm that David wrote of God's love for us as His creation. Miracles are what we hope for in life, and when they actually happen, we are filled with joy, expectancy, and gratefulness. This awe to believe there must be a Creator who cares and loves each one of us rises within our hearts. Life is a mystery to be lived, not knowing what will happen, and yet every one of us face new situations unfolding each day.

I choose to live each one of my days with a thankful heart. I am learning that trust is a channel through which peace can flow, winding its way to bless others with whom I come in contact. I became aware during my own Camino way; how can I be a miracle in someone else's life! I come daily before God and thank Him continually with a grateful heart for my life and ask that His peace will rule in my heart. Colossians 3:15. ESV

Something revolutionary occurs when we understand what it is to be continuously grateful. It rubs off on people and, when they recognize there is something different and special, it becomes contagious. Awe, and the awesomeness of resting in His peace is the most satisfying thing we all long for, especially in this fallen world.

In this day and age, people are looking for a quality of life that brings them purpose and peace. It seems that in our fast-paced society, there is a tendency to take control and strive for whatever it takes to become the top dog. Sometimes this is done at whatever cost, through manipulation and striving, bent at beating out the next one in line for position or gain. The world has changed so much out there, that the desire to stay at the top of the game has cost people their lives and the next generation seems misplaced and confused as to what it is they need.

I believe God has an order for our lives. His guidelines, found in the Bible, make clear that through honesty and hard work, we can find our purpose, and His purpose is served when we stay within His guidelines. It is simple and direct when we stay close to His word and apply His principles.

I look back and see that through my prayer, through my actions and through my giving how Abba Father has truly blessed me even during the storms of my life. And He has never left me nor forsaken me. Through His grace, He has guided me through every difficult time. He is a God of order, not conflict or chaos, a loving God who desires each one of us to rely on Him.

Hope Nugget: How amazing are Your thoughts towards me each day Abba.

WHEN LIFE WAS SIMPLE

Who would have thought forty years ago, how dramatically the world would change? I think about the days when I was a little girl, and that life was safe and easy and fun for the most part. I can remember the days; when I was a child, we would play a game in our town called 'Kick the Can.' In our small town, many of us kids would gather outdoors after supper. The game required an old can filled with rocks to make noise when we kicked it. The can was placed in the center of the street strategically known to be home base. We would chase the can and chase each other all over the place, trying to get the can back to home base.

I recall there were no cars in Ocean Falls BC back then, so it was a really safe place to live, surrounded by the Pacific Ocean and lots of forest and woodlands. In this game, all of us would run and hide and the person designated to be 'it' would close their eyes and count to fifty out loud, giving the rest of us time to find our hiding spots. The 'it,' person would search through the neighbourhood looking for someone to tag before any of us could make our way back to home base. Those that made it back safely could not be tagged, and the player that managed to get tagged then became the next person to be 'it.'

I loved this game and the community of kids older and younger than I who gathered to play. We would run through the streets hiding and stay up for hours in the early evening, tiring ourselves out before being called home to bed.

On many school grounds back in those days, we used to play another outdoor game called 'hopscotch.' Squares were drawn with chalk on the pavement in various patterns of one square then two and one and two and to finish with one square. Number one was placed in the first square then two and three and so on. Each girl had to hop on one foot, dropping a chain or marking to secure a spot on the hopscotch without touching the chalked lines. Girls in elementary schools all over the world played this simple game everywhere.

Do you remember 'Double Dutch?' A game with two skipping ropes and a person on each end twirling them in opposite directions. One or more of us would simultaneously jump to the rhythm of the ropes as they swirled without missing a beat and sometimes singing a tune while skipping. We laughed with glee and excitement as girls do at that age.

I remember being about eight years old when my family moved to Terrace BC to facilitate my father's practice. After school or during recess, we would gather to play marbles. It was one of my tomboy favourite games where, with a flick of your thumb and middle finger, a marble would shoot straight down the picnic table. If you had a keen eye, the marble would hit your opponent's, and that became your prize and you added it to the others you had collected. I remember my eyes would light up whenever I saw some over-sized marbles we called 'cobs' and the silver steel ones we called 'steeliest.' The object of the game was to snag as many unusual shaped marbles to add to your stash. In those days these marbles were some of my prized possessions, and now I wonder what happened to them. Some of my great childhood memories. Some of you reading this will smile, recalling similar days filled with outdoor activities and collective games.

What I loved about that time in my life was the outdoor camaraderie and the community of children gathering to play in the fresh air for hours and hours. It was a simple life; innocent and free as childhoods should be, filled with imagination and unrealistic dreams. I remember how family and friends gathered outside stoops and front yards to share stories and invest in each other's lives. Many of us, I recall, were from very large families that consisted of seven or eight children. There was always someone to play with.

Later on, in my early teen years, I remember the home telephone that had to be dialled. It would be attached to the wall in the kitchen, usually cream or yellow in color. When it rang, we would all run to answer it.

Those were the days that we teenage girls would chat with our high school girlfriends for hours and hours. Important conversations about clothes and boys with all the crazy emotional stuff young teenage girls go through. I think that still remains today. Of course, there were no cell phones back then, and you were lucky if there was another extension phone in the house to gain some privacy so other family members could not eavesdrop on those important teenage conversations.

Recently I forgot my cell phone at work one Friday afternoon as we were celebrating a co-worker's birthday. I was in a hurry to leave the office and left my phone on the table in the board room. It felt really weird having no communication with anyone, and I felt lost without my phone. I was at a friend's place that evening and had them text my kids and close friends to say I was okay, and I would figure out a way to retrieve my phone that weekend. Gone are the days of the 20th century when we had home phone lines when all we really needed was a cell phone. I ended up that weekend on social media with my laptop getting in touch with someone I work with to drive out to the office to pick up my cell phone. It's become like a psychological fix in our lives to be dependant on our cell-phones. How this world has changed!

Nowadays, we see people walking down the street, glued to their phones. I've seen some looking down and texting while walking into a crosswalk, oblivious as to what is going on around them. Driving on the busy freeway, I glance over as I pass a vehicle and someone will be texting on their cell phone. In an over-stimulated world, this activity of impatience is dangerous and careless. You can go to a restaurant and two people sitting across from each other, perhaps on a date, are looking down thumbing through their media rather than conversing together. One time I was in a coffee shop and sitting not too far from me was a group of young people sitting together. They were all looking down at their cell phones rather than having eye contact with each other and conversing.

Our children and grandchildren are growing up in an age where things are instant, and media stimulus is the norm. Interaction with one another is not as important as in my day when conversing with eye contact was the best inspiration for friendship and problem-solving.

We can be the examples by telling our own stories of adventure and explaining how hard work paid off after many years, so that we appreciate the things we wanted to accomplish and do. It wasn't instant gratification for many of us. It took time, patience, working hard, budgeting, setting goals, and accountability within a marriage and family to find our own rhythms in life.

I want to instill into my grandchildren one day the importance of time spent together, having conversations that will encourage them to also love others, be givers and appreciate what they have. Most of all, I urge them to value a love for God and family, be people who teach by example, pray much, express kindness, patience, and gentleness with their lives.

Each of us is on a journey that unfolds each day. Everyone's journey is different. We will affect people we come in contact with each day, and we will leave an impression of some kind. I want my mark to be one that represents the values and love that God has given me for others.

I've lived with care, courage and tenacity, and now I want to live each day continuing to impact others' lives through the experiences I have gained.

Let us continue as I share many more exciting undertakings of my travels, with Bert and on my own, that have impacted my life. These activities of exploring new horizons in various countries have taught me about purpose, risk, and being there at the right time to give hope in a much-needed situation. Learn about reflection, and the importance we can make in someone's life, whether it is in our own backyard or climbing a mountain in Spain.

DREAMING ON A
HAMMOCK

Eighteen years ago, my husband and I
had the privilege of going on a vacation to the
beautiful islands of Turks and Caicos. My
mom was gracious to look after our young
children to give us a much needed holiday
back then. The white sand, like powder
beneath our feet and the stunning crystal-clear
turquoise water lures you into the exoticness
of this oasis. Each day we would walk the
miles and miles of beach enjoying the beauty
surrounding us. One night after we walked
along the sandy shores, listening to the sound
of the ocean with the light breeze swaying the
palm trees, we came across a hammock strung
up between two palm trees. It was near the
beach so we could hear the roar of the waves
rushing back and forth as the tide slowly
changed.

We climbed up onto the hammock and
laid down on our backs looking up at the stars.
They seemed so bright against the clear sky.
We were dreamy-eyed, holding hands. The
beauty surrounding us was truly a tropical
hideaway. The warmth of our bodies next to
each other, the stars above so near, was a
dream come true. Away from the hustle and

bustle of everyday life. We were dreaming of the future, sharing our thoughts, and committing our plans to God, trusting Him to orchestrate each one of our hearts' desires.

Bert wanted to work less in construction so that he could focus more on writing music. He was passionate about music, and it having an impact on others. He wanted to put out another album, and we hoped for more ministry opportunities to encourage people through music and the arts. It was a wonderful time together, and I recognized that each time we were able to get away, Bert was relaxed and able to come up with fresh ideas for songs. He was free to be, and through the quietness of his soul, he was creative, able to fly, formulate and compose new music.

When our vacation was over, and we were back to our routines of daily living at home, our prayers were answered. We were fortunate to hire a super foreman to help manage our construction jobs, and that enabled Bert to work one day less each week. His love for writing music produced the albums 'Dream,' 'Seven Songs,' and 'Lights and Oceans' over the years. I look back at the many fond memories of releasing our faith and eventually seeing the substance of those things we were hoping for become a reality.

On this dream getaway, one of my fond memories was the fun we had going out on a boat tour, visiting the various Caicos islands and the small cays. One of the guides on the ship had a spear on a rope hung over his shoulder, and he would dive into the ocean to the bottom of the sea holding his breath for about 20 seconds to bring up conch shells for those of us who wanted one. Each one of us on the tour would jump into the warm water, snorkelling the blue, green waters and watch for our guide and as he came up. Each one of us touched his hand in order for him to legally bring the conch to the surface. He would dive down and come back up to the surface to meet us one by one with a conch shell.

Later that afternoon we sailed to a beautiful abandoned beach to clean out our treasured shells and the boat captain cooked up a wonderful conch salad for our group. It was like an experience out of a movie, resting on your own abandoned island in the warmth of the sun, having a barbecue amongst the tropical islands near the Bahamas. We experienced a dream come true.

AUSTRALIA

My life these past few years has been pretty incredible. I have done things I never ever imagined I would do in my lifetime. Two years ago in November, I got on an airplane by myself for the first time since Bert's passing and flew all the way to beautiful Australia. That was a brave move for me. It was our winter here and a nasty one that year, so to walk along the Wollongong beach in the early summer mornings with my good friends Ken and April was a dream come true.

We would get up at 6 am and have our coffee. Then we'd slip away to walk and pray with the sound of the ocean nearby before the heat of the sun was upon us. Our daily power walks on the sandy beach and sacred times with our heavenly Father were intimate moments. The three of us had a really special time, living in close quarters for five weeks and doing life together.

They were a part of a Youth With A Mission organization, and I had the privilege of visiting the base. April invited me to accompany her to encourage and pray for the many young people that were attending the school there. It was an incredible privilege to speak into these young people's lives and to encourage them with hopeful expectations for their futures infused with God's love.

On one special outing, we took Ken and April's grandkids to a zoo in the area near where they lived. It was pretty exciting to see many exotic birds, including the Laughing Kookaburra bird with its long beak and cackling laughter unique to the sounds of Eastern Australia.

I remember growing up with the classic song:

Kookaburra sits in the old gum tree
Merry merry king of the bush is he
Laugh, Kookaburra, laugh Kookaburra
Gay your life must be

Kookaburra sits in the old gum tree
Eating all the gumdrops he can see
Stop, Kookaburra, Stop, Kookaburra
Leave some there for me

Kookaburra sits in the old gum tree
Counting all the monkeys he can see
Stop, Kookaburra
That's no monkey, that's me.

I remember singing that funny little song over and over in my kindergarten class many, many years ago. The song was written by Marion Sinclair back in 1932.

Hope Nugget: **Laughter is medicine for your soul.**

Kookaburra

ONE OF A KIND MAMMALS

Something you don't get to experience here in Canada is seeing kangaroos hopping across a field or actually seeing one up close as we did at the zoo outside Wollongong. I remember driving with my friends one day, seeing a herd of them bouncing in unison across a pasture. They can leap up to 30 miles per hour. These unique creatures are indigenous to Australia. It was a sight to see them at the zoo and realize how agile they are. They can jump 30 or more feet in one bounding hop. When standing upright, they are over six feet tall and use their long tails for balance. Female kangaroos have a fold in the front of their stomachs to carry baby kangaroos called Joeys.

It was special to take in the sites and to enjoy the rugged beauty of this beautiful land. One of the engineers I work with, Drew, grew up in Australia and eventually emigrated to Canada many years later. Before I ventured to the coastlands of his country, he told me stories about his early life. When he was growing up, he would regularly shake out his shoes each day in case a deadly spider had made it's home in his boots the night before. Australia has some of the deadliest spiders in the world: The Sydney funnel-web spider, the

Redback spider, the Trapdoor spider, the
Mouse spider, and of course the Tarantula.

Australia has other very dangerous
animals residing there, like the Eastern brown
snake, Box jellyfish, Bull shark, saltwater or
estuarine crocodiles, just to name a few. I was
careful to keep my eyes open and found
myself shaking out my sandals if I left them
outside. Drew told me that it was like
anything else - if you provoke these creatures
they will attack you, and if you mind your
business you won't have a run-in with them.

Regardless of knowing the history about
the deadliest creatures in Australia, it was very
enjoyable to observe the uniqueness and
beauty of the wildlife. Dingoes, kangaroos,
and koala bears are associated with this
country, but I especially liked the exotic birds
with their vibrant colors. We saw king parrots,
crested cockatoos, magpies, crimson rosella,
and the laughing Kookaburra.

KOALA BEAR

One of the cutest sights at the zoo was seeing a koala digesting on eucalyptus leaves. These grey fury mammals are marsupials, like kangaroos. They are not bears as some people think. Koalas have strong clawed feet so that they can cling to the branches of trees. Like the kangaroo the females also have flaps in their bodies to carry their young in a pouch. They can eat up to two pounds of eucalyptus leaves a day, storing some of the leaves as a snack in their cheeks. From eating so much of the eucalyptus leaves, the moisture they retain allows them not to have to drink much water. They like to sleep a lot, and Koalas will climb into the branches and fall asleep for up to 18 hours a day. The zoo keeper allowed us to have our pictures taken with one and she had to pry its sharp claws away from the hideaway to enable it to sit straight up on a post for stability. Up close this furry little cutie looked dazed, probably from stuffing his face with so many leaves. It was a great experience to learn about kangaroos and koalas, two marsupials native to Australia.

Koala

kangaroo

THE GREAT BARRIER REEF

It was summertime in rugged and beautiful Australia. I thought I would take advantage of my time here to see the sights. Australia is a large spread out country like Canada, running 3,700 km from North to South and 4,000 km from east to west. For the most part, flying rather than driving is a more practical way of getting around, especially when you are on a time schedule.

Ken helped me book a flight to Queensland in north-eastern Australia. My purpose was to snorkel along the magnificent Great Barrier Reef, a World Heritage site. I really hoped that once underwater, I would find 'Nemo,' an orange and black striped clownfish that was a character in the movie 'Finding Nemo.'

The group I was snorkelling with covered a large section of the reef. We all were in awe of the many colourful fish, coral, and sea life in this beautiful underwater world. Eventually, some of us did find 'Nemo!' I was surprised to see how small this fish was. Known as the false clownfish, Nemo and his species live around sea anemones who provide protection and leftovers for them to eat. In return, the clownfish bring food to the anemones and also provide cleaning and remove parasites for them. The clownfish and the sea anemones become a unique pair of species, helping each other to thrive in a mutual beneficial relationship beneath the sea. A dream came true for me as I snorkelled the world-renowned and very beautiful reef to find 'Nemo!'

Teresa with flippers and gear

55

Great Barrier Reef and Australian flag

Photo of a portion of the Great Barrier Reef

Photo of Teresa snorkeling

MAGNIFICENT AYERS ROCK

During my time in Aussie land, my friends and I flew up to Uluru, in the Northern Territories, to see the magnificent Ayers Rock. Another one of the great natural wonders that you won't find anywhere else on our planet. It is a beautiful red massive sandstone rock in the middle of nowhere. It's in an arid desert situated in the Uluru–Tjuta National Park. The caves, sand dunes, and various patterns reflect the rains and winds that have shaped it over time. Ayers Rock is sacred to the indigenous people living in Uluru, and they protect and guard the welfare of the park. It has been a sacred landmark to them throughout their centuries of residence in the area.

You don't want to miss the sunlight highlighting the colors of rock at sunrise and sunset. You'll see a stunning ochre brown, an incredible orange and then a startling red. People from all over the world were up early, with their expensive cameras taking photos to catch a glimpse of this amazing view of the sunlight passing over the rock. We experienced an unusual number of stormy days when we were there, as that time of the year is usually known for its extremely hot temperatures. Because of the cooler weather, the conditions were bearable for us to explore the natural beauty of Ayers rock.

While we were there we decided to walk around the base of the rock; a well-marked 12 km walk displaying the unusual eucalyptus gum trees, shrubs, reptiles, birds, dingoes, and insects of all kinds. We felt so small walking along the path next to the massiveness of this structure. Stopping to visit ancient watering holes and lush woodlands gives you an idea of the cultural significance, and historical rock formations created over the centuries. The sounds of the rare wildlife and the smells and beauty of the exotic species of native plants were breathtaking. The vibrant colors of the various plants: red, blue, yellow and orange popped out amongst the wooded hue. This was one of the most amazing, natural and once-in-a-lifetime experiences I had.

Hope Nugget: Have faith and step out of your comfort zone.

Ayers Rock
Uluru-Kata Tjuta National Park

AIRBORNE AGAIN TO
BRAZIL

On New Years eve of 2017, I was sitting in the Vancouver airport getting ready to fly out on a rather risky, yet exciting adventure to Brazil. That's where my friends Dan and Sandy were house-sitting for some friends. They had invited me to come and hang out with them for a few weeks in João Pessoa, a coastal city in eastern Brazil.

Before I boarded my plane at YVR, I got a strong impression that 2018 was going to be a year of new beginnings, breakthroughs and blessings. It was a word I felt would resonate hope to many people that I knew were looking for the much-needed breakthroughs in this broken world. I sensed a coming of the restoration we all long for. Each one of us passing through this life is on a journey through the ups and downs that come our way. There is a need for us to release the faith to believe for those breakthroughs and blessings that Abba wants to give us.

I was stepping out into the unknown again, scared yet hoping this next venture would bring some more healing and adventure into my life. Waiting to board my flight, I was pondering the fact that keeping myself busy is good, but not to avoid pain in my life. I knew that by getting away on this trip, I would receive good advice from some very special counsellors. I was sure these friends would speak encouragement and wisdom into my life. This bold move to fly to an unfamiliar country did have me on my toes. Yet, I knew my friends would be there to greet me.

I flew to Sao Paulo then on to João Pessoa. This city is known as the place where the sun rises first, because it is located in the easternmost part of the Americas, 34° 47' 38" West, 7° 9' 28" South. Its easternmost point is known as Ponta do Seixas. When the sun sets at night over the water, it looks like a beautiful orange ball sitting right in front of you. You can imagine reaching out and almost touching it from where you are standing on the boardwalk along the beach. Another stunning wonder that left me in awe.

I did not know the Portuguese language, so it was a bit of challenge. When I arrived at the international airport in Sao Paulo, I made my way to the domestic airport to find someone who could speak English. I followed my heart and headed into the unknown to find the right gate for my flight to João Pessoa. Dan had reminded me that anything could happen, and a gate change could occur at the last minute. After a long layover that day, my gate did change at the last minute, and I went running down the stairs to find my domestic flight leaving two hours later than expected. Eventually, I arrived after a long day of flying and I walked out through the doors, delighted to see my friends, as they were relieved to see me.

The wonderful beauty of this part of Brazil was spectacular. Beaches everywhere and a Latin culture with charming, unique sounds and rhythms. Another 'Buen Camino' adventure.

Dan, Sandy, and I had the privilege to see God in action in a home-church gathering one night. Wellington, a young worship leader from Brazil, led songs with passion and though I did not know the Portuguese language, it didn't matter because when hearts are knit together to worship Jesus, that is all that matters. I was able to minister to his wife about being married to a musician and finding the balance between ministry and family life. She was really grateful. I knew what she was going through, raising a young family with a husband who had been given opportunities to do music ministry in various settings and countries.

I noticed that there was a hunger amongst the younger generation in João Pessoa to see God move in Spirit and in truth. They were hungry for God and to see Him move in their country amongst their people groups. God is able to do so much more than we could ever ask or think; we just have to believe that and give away His hidden treasure, namely His love for others.

In Brazil we did not go out at night because of the high crime rate. It's good to know, though, that the Holy Spirit is moving there.

He has His willing vessels shining their lights, ministering to the prostitutes on the beach areas not far from where we were staying. The people whose home we were staying at were away visiting family in Canada. When they are back in Brazil, they have amazing hearts that reflect kindness on a regular basis to the street girls in that area. Many of the young women are forced into prostitution because of poverty. The back alleyways near the beach is where they turn their tricks.

The couple from Canada for whom we were house-sitting, put together toiletry packages for the girls and they always set up a tent on the beach for them to avoid the hot sun. They invite the girls to come and speak with them, and it is a place where they are safe. Trust is built and eventually the girls learn about God's love through this couple. Some of the girls have turned their lives around, gotten jobs and, moved to find safe places to live. This couple is love in action.

There is a revolution of truth amongst the young Brazilians I met, who are passionate to share Christ's love in João Pessoa.

Fishing Village

At the Paraiba river with Dan and Sandy

ISRAEL

In my four years since Bert passed, I have been experiencing grateful opportunities to go and explore the beauty of some incredible countries and mix with uniquely diverse cultures. One of these was my visit to the nation of Israel in the Spring of 2018.

After Christmas 2017, my good friends Joyce and Gary let me live with them for three months when I downsized from my house to a new townhouse that was being built for me. The trades were so busy in 2016 that it took three months longer than expected for it to be ready for me to move in and they graciously let me live with them. During one of our cups of coffee and prayer times in the morning, Joyce and I got talking about places we wanted to go and visit. Of course, Israel was one place we always desired to go and experience. My Canadian friends Dan and Sandy who had lived and taught in Israel previously for many years, recommended some people to go with. A year later, I found myself flying to Tel Aviv with a group of 24 from the B.C. lower mainland and one couple from Saskatchewan.

How do I describe my time in Israel?

When people have asked me that question, I reflect and almost don't know what to say because it is such a private experience for anyone who goes to visit this tiny nation. There is something magical about the land, the various cultures, the history, and the biblical truths. The feeling you get when you are there is different from any normal experience.

To walk amongst the historical ruins of empires, layered upon each other, which have come and gone over thousands and thousands of years is amazing. You can get to stand on the shore by the sea of Galilee, and reflect upon the scriptures in the Bible that tell of Jesus calming the rough seas and Peter having faith to step out of the boat and walk on water. You can visit the grassy hill where the five tiny loaves and two fish fed more than 5000 people. You can reflect upon the humble, triumphant entry of Jesus into Jerusalem as the Prince of Peace.

It was surreal as I stood and imagined how so many biblical references took place here. My friend Joyce and I were fascinated in so many ways as we walked along the Via Dolorosa in Jerusalem, imagining the painful pilgrimage Jesus took to the cross.

When we went to the town of Magdala, where Mary Magdalene was from, I was touched deeply. I thought of how she was once an outcast and how she had turned her life around and traveled with Jesus as one of his followers, witnessing his crucifixion, burial, and resurrection.

My friend James and his wife were in Israel, leading Garden Tomb tours. On the very last day of their tour, before heading back to Canada, our group was able to meet them and experience James' passion for Christ. We were impacted deeply by the stories he shared about the specialness of the place where the body of Jesus was laid after His death and burial in the garden tomb. There were a few tears in our group as James shared his own personal testimony, as well as some history about the garden tomb. For me, it was nice to see a familiar face again from home.

We went to the Western Wall, also known as the Wailing Wall, and placed our prayers written on pieces of paper, amongst the ancient stone bricks.

We walked through the old city in Jerusalem, divided into four quarters and saw Christians, Muslims, Jews, and Armenians living together. It was remarkable and so diversely unique. We explored the markets where the vendors sold their wares. The incredible colors and smells and the variety of spices sold by the local vendors was amazing. There were so many things I learned, not only historically but culturally, each day as we travelled from Tel Aviv to Eliot in the south near Jordan.

You could spend months in Israel exploring the cave where David hid from Saul, the caves where the ancient scrolls were found and Jaffa from where Jonah sailed on his tumultuous journey.

Masada was a magnificent, yet heart-wrenching experience. Here was one of the northern palaces that Herod the Great built high upon a cliff. He never occupied it. He died an unruly death before it was completed. I work for an engineering firm, and I was amazed by the engineering minds in those days. They created a way for water from the mountains to run down and through trenches to be stored in 12 huge cisterns in the insulated walls within this desert area. I was in awe of the infrastructure and ingenious minds who designed the three palaces strategically laid out by Herod: Roman baths and public storehouses. The years and the manpower it took to erect this citadel was astounding. In 70 AD, a group of Jewish rebels fled from Roman occupation to hide out in Masada. The Romans built a huge ramp with a battering ram to destroy the fortress and capture the 960 souls living there. The leaders of the community convinced the members to draw lots to take their lives rather than become Roman slaves. When the Romans eventually entered the fortress, they found Masada deserted except for two women and five children who were hiding in one of the rooms. The fall of this magnificent city was the final act in the Roman conquest of Judea. I was impacted by the story our Jewish guide shared of Masada. It was a lot for me to process.

From there we went to the Dead Sea, where we covered ourselves with the minerals in the mud and then floated in the concentrated salt water. Our skin was so silky smooth, better than a spa treatment, after we rinsed off the mud. Israel, on so many levels. Israel is a country filled with mystery and controversy. It is the Holy Land and our heavenly Father Abba has his hand upon it. No matter what has occurred over the centuries, people are drawn to Israel. Sometimes it is impossible to understand or explain why, yet for me, since my experience visiting, I read the scriptures in a new light. Bible verses come to light because I have trekked where Jesus walked, and I have seen where He and His disciples and followers lived. I have been to the many towns and cities mentioned in the Bible and visibly read the verses with an excitement and new understanding. This Camino trek inspired me to continue to pray for the peace of Jerusalem and all that God has intended for the people groups living in this tiny country.

Standing by the Sea of Galilee

Floating on the Dead Sea

Caesarea Philippi

Masada

Tristram's Starling

NEVER ALONE

Sometimes I just don't see
There's so much more
Sometimes I just don't feel it
The way I should

There's a river in my soul
And I'm never alone. Woo oh oh.
Feel the higher ground
Feel his love around
It's like a river and it's coming down
It's really coming down

Do te do do do do. Do te do do do do ah yeah.

It's like a river and it's coming down
It's really coming down
It's really coming down

Do te do do do do. Do te do do do do yeah.
Oh oh

It's like a river and it's coming down
It's really coming down. It's really coming
down.

Bert Petkau Lights & Oceans
CD 2014

THE CAMINO: HOW IT ALL STARTED

In the early Spring of 2018, I met my two high school girlfriends for tea to discuss possibly going on a trek from northern France into Spain. The trek is called, "El Camino de Santiago," and in English it means "The Way of Saint James." We were intrigued with walking a part of the way because of our limited time schedules and thus began to plan our journey set for September 11th, 2018.

The three of us were approaching significant birthdays in August and early September of 2018 and thought this would be a great way to celebrate. In 2014, when my husband released his last album, my girlfriends had never met him, and I invited them to his big event. They were delighted to come out from the city to observe a part of my life they never knew, as each one of our lives after high school went in different directions. The nice thing was Debbie and Moira were childhood friends and neighbors, so they had kept in touch over the years. Moira and I reconnected on social media five years ago.

In September of 2017, before our Camino walk, I was amazed how Moira and her sister and eight other guys bravely tackled a hike along the West Coast Trail on the south-western edge of Vancouver Island. It is part of the Pacific Rim National Park, open from May to the end of September, and you have to reserve a spot ahead of time to hike it.

Compared to the Camino de Santiago, the West Coast Trail is 75 km is a lesser walk in mileage, but much more difficult than the trail we were planning on pursuing. To go on the West Coast Trail, you have to bring all of your supplies, including food, cooking utensils and a tent and even your own toilet paper. There are no washrooms or showers, and it is a true 'roughing it' experience amongst the beautiful coastline of British Columbia.

Moira had conquered the West Coast Trail, and though she is a tiny little thing, she could walk circles around me on the Camino. She is a strong woman, and when we needed our own time alone on the trail, there she was, steady and sure as she walked ahead of me. She motivated me to put one foot in front of the other, even in moments when I was too tired to keep on keeping on.

In the Spring of 2018, I got together with my friend Sherry Koop to go over details of what was expected on the Camino trail. Sherry and her husband Wes were leaving Canada to run a café right on the Camino path in the quaint town of Vianna, Spain in May of 2018. She gave me incredible detailed information as what to bring and what to expect on this walk.

When the three of us girls got together beforehand, the checklist I brought with me that day was really helpful as we did not know what to expect. We decided to ask a friend of Moira's to book our travel itinerary. We arranged for a company to pick up and transport each of our suitcases from place to place. That was a smart move, as there was no way I could have carried more than a light backpack with necessities and two metal water canisters when we were climbing some of the steepest hills on the sometimes arduous journey in Spain. We met people along the way who had too much stuff, and they either mailed items back to their homes or did the same as we did and hired a company to take their luggage from town to town.

There was an eye-catching scenic movie made about ten years ago based on a true story about an optometrist's son who went to France to start his Camino walk and fell and died in the Pyrenees mountains where we were planning to walk the same route. The beautifully filmed movie is called "The Way" with Martin Sheen and his son Emilio Estevez. Martin, playing the part of the father, goes to retrieve his son's body and rather than returning to America decides to walk the Camino de Santiago in his son's place.

The three of us sat down and watched the movie before we left and we loved it. Looking back now, I remember so many places I either stayed at, walked past and recognized where various scenes of this great movie were filmed.

Hope Nugget: Accomplishments in life are the difficulties we face and the ones we conquer.

THE SCALLOP SHELL

The symbol of the Camino de Santiago is what is referred to as 'The Vieira.' In Galician and Spanish, it means "scallop shell." This ionic symbol leads pilgrims to find their way to Santiago. Apparently, there are many legends, myths and stories that are connected to the 'Vieira,' and the Saint James Way.

One legend is that the ship carrying St. James' body was destroyed in a storm, and his body was discovered on the shore undamaged because many, many scallop shells covered him.

Another myth is that the shell has a metaphorical meaning, when you look at the lines (usually yellow coming out of a dark blue background,) they represent the different routes that the pilgrims take to guide them to safety when they arrive at the tomb of Saint James in Santiago de Compostela. Many pilgrims see the lines on the shell as a reflection of many paths leading to one point.

Back in the early days, the scallop shell was worn as a symbol by medieval pilgrims, attached to a hat they wore, or on their cloaks. It also had a practical purpose. It was used as a bowl to hold food or a cup to drink from during the pilgrimage. At churches or gatherings, it was used to feed the pilgrims en route. The shell was used to measure food along the way in kitchens when given out to those that were hungry.

After reaching Santiago, many pilgrims continued on to the coast to a place that is now called Finisterre. It was believed that this was the end of the earth, '*Finis*' meaning end and '*Terre*' meaning earth. Here they would collect scallop shells from the ocean. The shell was a symbol of the right way to Santiago de Compostela and proof the route had been completed. My scallop shell sits on the table in my dining area at home, reminding me of the feat I have accomplished.

Shell and Camino passport

Camino Passport Stamped Each Day

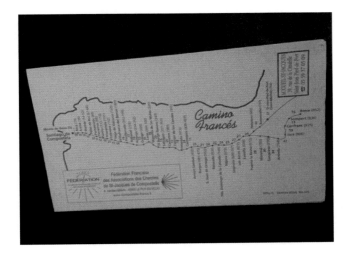

Camino Route Starting in St. Jean Pied, France

THE BEAUTIFUL PYRENEES MOUNTAINS

We left Vancouver on September 11, 2018, and flew to Madrid and then on to San Sabastian to rest for a few days before trekking and to get over our jetlag. My friend Sherry and one of the engineers I work with, suggested I go to San Sebastian, Spain. It is a beautiful resort town in Spain's Basque Country surrounded by beautiful beaches. Tired from the long day of travel, we found our way into the old city. We walked the beaches, enjoyed tapas, walked up to the old fort and admired the sailboats in the harbour and the beauty of this gem of a hideaway.

A couple of days later we got our bus tickets to make our way up to Saint Jean de Pied in France, where we would be starting our walk. On September 14[th,] 2018, we started our adventure. Rested up and having registered, the three of us rose early to start our trek and enjoy the quaintness of this town.

We were told from the start; the hardest part of the Camino walk was venturing through the Pyrenees mountains. We did not know what to expect, and so off we started into the unknown on a clear day, with blue skies and a gorgeous sun. It is often foggy in the mountain, but we missed it and heard that a day later, the fog had settled in. We were able to enjoy the majesty of this mountain range for miles and miles on a warm sunny day. In the distance, you could hear bells, as we walked past sheep, horses running wild and cattle settling in the meadows. As we got near these animals, we could see that bells were tied around each of their necks, markings I suppose for their owners.

We stopped in a little café up the mountain, meeting many others pilgrims on our first day. I remember the lady we registered with telling us that 400 people had signed up to do the Camino the same day we did and that many more were to sign up the days following.

We chatted with so many folks along the way who were delighted to find out what country and city we were all from. Many of the conversations helped to pass the time as we climbed higher and higher over the mountain range, cheering each other on through the steep terrain. Nine and one-half hours later, we were exhausted. We had walked 20km up the Pyrenees mountain range, seven km down and another three into Roncesvalles. We were now in Spain.

We showered and went down for our pilgrim supper with others staying at our hotel, relieved we made it through the first day. Later I soaked my sore feet and lathered ointment on them. Then, spent with fatigue, I fell into bed for a much-needed rest and slept like a baby that night.

Heading out on the first day

Climbing up the Pyrenees mountains

Sheep and the bells around their necks

Teresa taking a break in the Pyrenees Mountains climb

Water break on the way to Zubiri

Now that we were officially in Spain, we got up early the next morning, eager to start our Camino walk. On that day our destination was Zubiri, 22 km away. Feeling like we had accomplished much the day before, we were determined to march through the next few weeks with a mission accomplished mindset. No more make-up, heels or mascara! It was time to focus on important things like looking out for our feet, reserving our energy, and treading safely to stay on track as we conquered the arduous climb. This enabled us to enjoy the beautiful scenery through the Pyrenees. When I got up that morning to start our second day, I recognized the inn we stayed at in Roncesvalles was one of the buildings that was filmed in the movie I mentioned, "The Way."

We were ready early on day two to start the journey and we crossed the street to take a photo of the three of us standing by a sign that reads 790 km to Santiago. Probably thousands have taken pictures right there. After crossing the street, Debbie fell and was seriously hurt. We did not know how badly at the time. We sat on the sidewalk for about 20 minutes in disbelief. She thought she felt ok, so we decided to start our trek to Zubiri. We walked through the countryside with its long outstretched meadows into a wooded, tranquil forest with the Pyrenees mountains as a backdrop slowly slipping past us. Halfway through the forest, we stopped for a break and took our shoes and socks off, munched on a power bar and drank some water to stay hydrated.

On our first day in the mountains, we had met Lucy from England and this day we met up with her again. I walked with her a bit and found out that her mom had passed from cancer a year before and she was doing the walk to find a special place to spread her ashes with her sister the following year. She was planning on walking all 790 km and had taken a month and a half off to do the trek.

790 to Santiago, first day in Spain

The inn we stayed at in Roncesvalles on our first night,
where they filmed the movie "The Way."

Café en route

Ancient Fountain water fill up.

We soon became social media friends and I had the privilege to walk two extra days with her when Moira decided to spend a few days with Debbie near the end of our excursion.

On the route from Roncesvalles to Zubiri the paths that descend are very long and pronounced with many uphill ramps. Oaks, pine and beech trees line the wooded slopes that eventually lead to the top of Erro, a charming town located in the community of Navarra, in northern Spain. On this day we realized we would cross two mountain passes, Alto de Mezquiriz as well as the Alto de Erro, before descending to the village of Zubiri.

Trekking through these passes, the paths were so steep that I thought I wouldn't make it and this was only my second day on the Camino. Everything in me wanted to quit. My leg muscles were screaming, my calves were burning, and inside my mind, I prayed, "Abba I need your help because this is much harder than I expected."

As I pressed my walking sticks into the ground to climb the steep terrain, within me, I saw a picture of a shepherd and how he would use the staff to guide the sheep into a pasture for safety. For me, it meant to lean on the staff and, as I pushed through the burden of climbing, the pain lessened because Jesus was my Shepherd, helping me to overcome. I saw a picture of Jesus falling while He carried the cross to Calvary for me. When the Roman soldier was scourging Him, I had a vision of Jesus kneeling, looking up into the eyes of Veronica and, as she wiped His bloodstained face with a cloth, He received comfort to continue carrying the cross. I saw the tenderness in His eyes now looking at me, with an everlasting peace urging me on to run my race. I thought to myself if Jesus could carry that cross, be crucified for my sins, pierced, whipped, and have nails pounded into

His flesh for my sake, how much more could I make it over some of these painstaking hills. I had tears in my eyes: my heart was beating out of my chest, and as I stood at the top of the cliff to catch my breath and rest, I was relieved. The Good Shepherd was by my side.

Jesus met me in my need on a dusty trail in the middle of Spain, rooting for me, believing in me, standing with me. Soon, a quiet confidence rose up inside my spirit, because I believed that if Abba was on my side, I could do anything.

I have been given the privilege to be His hands and feet to a hurting world. This is extravagant love that was purchased for my life and yours, 2000 years ago. It was a reminder for me to carry on with contagious hope of His love for me and to give it away to others as I traveled on. He is the Good Shepherd, and we are to lean on His staff.

He lives in me, and He is the peace that can only fill the emptiness in our hearts. Nothing else can. We are spirit, and it is the Holy Spirit with our spirits that truly brings life out of brokenness and restoration. When I purpose to love God with all of my heart, soul, and mind — that is when He gives me the courage to face life fearlessly. It is His power that enables me to do that, not on my own strength but in His strength.

We are not to recoil from afflictions or hardships. They are part of the journey that shape and mold us into who we are. I don't want to do meaningless things with my life, and on this trip, I had a lot of time to spend in quietness as I walked, and to be in communication with God.

> *I will instruct you and teach you in the way you should go; I will counsel you with My eye upon you.* Psalm 32:8 ESV.

Ask Him, in the quietness of your days, to show you what He has planned for your life, and stay in the place of rest that He offers to each one of us when we get weary. With one foot in front of the other and His marching orders, we can finish each one of our races.

We stopped for a water break again and sat in the forest with our shoes and socks nearby to give our feet some air and a much-needed rest.

Our last descent to Zubiri is known as one of the most difficult and dangerous of the French Way, because of the steepness along the cliffs. Sharp, loose, uneven stones of all shapes and sizes were everywhere. This is where sprains, strains, and injuries occur most often down the 4 km slope. As we hiked down the steep wooded landscape, Lucy allowed Debbie to lean on her for support for her wrecked ankle. Lucy was like a steadfast staff and one of our Camino angels.

I remember that day how my knees were hurting as we walked down the steep terrain. My walking sticks that my boss Jenny lent me came in handy for stability. We soon saw in the distance the 12th-century medieval bridge (La Rabia) with a lovely stream running beneath it. Our feet stinging, Moira and I walked down to the stream and took off our socks and shoes, welcoming the refreshing ice-cold water to soak in the achiness of many kilometres we had covered that day.

Earlier, on the path, we had met a couple from Ireland. Eileen was a nurse, and she and her husband took our friend Debbie to the hospital, as Moira and I had another 6 km to walk to get to our hotel.

We found out later Debbie was badly injured and she could not continue the walk with us. It was a pretty emotional time for all three of us. Can you imagine how she had come all that way to Spain with excitement and anticipation, and now she was not able to carry on her Camino journey. It was truly devastating. Through mixed emotions, Debbie bravely decided to take the bus from place to place to finish her walk in a different way. Moira and I continued on for the remaining weeks, our emotions being pulled to finish what we started. To be honest, it was really difficult, but I chose not to let the disappointment hinder what was ahead of me. I had to finish what I came to do.

Our hotel host in Zubiri was Joseph. He shared at dinner with Moira and me that his hotel was used for filming another portion of "The Way" where Martin Sheen meets another pilgrim, a Canadian woman on their journey to Santiago de Compostela.

Joseph's hotel from the movie "The Way"

Those of us from North America were surprised by the unusual September temperatures in this part of Spain. We were expecting to walk in a cooler climate and found we were walking in 90 degrees Fahrenheit (or 32 plus Celsius) with little or no shade most days. I was thankful for the brimmed hat I had brought, the sunglasses and lots of sunscreen. There were many days when we walked miles upon miles through the heat, grateful to find a tree to hide behind to rest our weary feet and to stay hydrated. What was more tiring for the two of us, was not so much the trek, but the exhaustion from the heat of the sun beating down upon us each day. We did our best to stay hydrated as we walked through scrubby grass trails and rocky terrain.

HIS LOVE IS OVER ME

I am weak I am Faint with love
Strengthen me again with Your love
Lead me near to Your side
To the one that my heart loves.

Chorus:
'Cause Your love is ever over me Oh – Oh
Oh Your mercy Your love is ever over me.

Winter is past the rains are gone
Flowers do appear again
The sounds of singing lead me along
To the one that my heart loves.

Bridge:
I am weak I am faint with love
Strengthen me again with Your love
Lead me near lead me to Your side
To the one that my heart loves.

Bert Petkau Seven Songs CD
2011

ZUBIRI TO PAMPLONA

The next morning. we walked alongside the river Arda for many miles (kilometres), as we focused on reaching our next destination. The largest city along the French Way, known as Pamplona, was 24 km away. As we made our way over a bridge, we trudged into the village of Akerreta to stop for a morning latte. I loved how every town was centered around a church with the big black bell or bells ringing in the distance. In these little towns, tidy, colourful geraniums lined wrought-iron balconies outside each home, demonstrating a sense of pride. After meandering for many more miles, we passed a quarry on the left-hand side.

In the distance, we could see another ancient bridge, the "Magdalena Bridge," known as the Pilgrims' main entrance leading into the large city of Pamplona. We walked through some of the city outskirts eventually turning left to walk parallel, along the Park of La Media Luna. Moira had a map of the city to guide us as we wandered through the streets. It seemed we were walking in circles as we tried to find our hotel. It was like when you are looking for your sunglasses and can't find them, only to discover they are sitting on your forehead. I eventually looked up from the map to read a sign, and there was our hotel, right in front of us! We had circled the block many times trying to pinpoint it.

Dinner, window shopping and walking through the square — was how we enjoyed our time in Pamplona. I had a nice balcony outside my room, and while the sun was shining, I washed a few pairs of my Moreno wool socks and some clothing to lay out to dry on the patio ledge.

We got up the next morning to continue our routine, leaving the large city of Pamplona early. We walked 5km just to get through the vast city before arriving at the trail that was to take us to the next village of Cizur Menor. The route is mixed with lots of countryside meadows that line busy, country highways.

Walking along the park that morning, we met up with a couple of familiar faces, Bill and his step-son Ron, who were from Calgary. We had registered together on the same day in France, and we were delighted to meet up with our fellow Canadian friends again. The time went by quickly as we made conversation along the way and as Bill shared an interesting story about the 12th-century church of San Miguel in Cizur Menor. It is known for the chivalry of the Knights of St. John of Malta, who aided pilgrims and protected them from war-torn escapades in that century. The Pope Pascall 2nd recognized the protective mission work of the Knights of Malta knights as they provided aid and safety for the pilgrims and honoured them for their efforts.

Wrought iron window boxes

Our next uphill challenge that day would be the Alto del Perdon. Some will know it as the "Hill of Forgiveness." It would be the hardest ascent of the day with views at the top that are breathtaking. Windmills churn along the top of the hill and farmland dotted with hay bales can be seen for miles. It was quite a climb, and when we reached the top, we came across the sculpture of pilgrims that is portrayed in the movie "The Way." The iconic sculpture has graced this summit since 1996. Words inscribed in Spanish mean, "Where the path of the wind crosses with that of the stars." There is a story portrayed about the famous figures. You can go on-line and read about the pilgrimages and what they represent - various times from the Middle Ages to this present day. I was told that Martin Sheen did not climb the steep hill to film his scene here in the movie "The Way." He took a taxi to the sculpture!

We caught our breath and took a photo stop before we headed downward to the steep rocky descent on the next leg of our passage, carefully placing our footing along the loose craggy rocks.

Top of the Hill of Forgiveness

On our path that day we walked through a few
more small Spanish villages again lined with
colourful planters and wrought-iron balconies.
It was another scorching hot day and we were
grateful to stop at an ancient fountain with
markings indicating that it was built in 1020.
We each filled our water bottles and stopped
to soak our feet in the refreshing cold water. I
still remember sitting on the edge of the
ancient fountain enjoying the foot bath and
some shade. With another 5km to go, we soon
arrived to our destination in Puenta La Reina
and received a stamp on our Camino
passports. We had a shower and supper and,
tired yet relieved, we met up with some other
friends we met earlier from England and
Ireland. These ladies were childhood friends
reuniting to do a part of the walk together like
us.

Grateful for ice cold water

Ancient Fountain est. 1021

Enroute to Puente la Reina

As we journeyed on to Estella, we met a father and son from England walking the Camino together. I thought how special it was to walk the path with one of your children. It was such a great achievement. They told us they had brought too much stuff with them in their backpacks and it made the walk difficult. When they reached Pamplona a few days earlier, they unloaded their packs and shipped some of their heavier items back home to

England. I was glad we had our luggage go ahead of us each day, and realized you really didn't need a lot of clothing on a trek like this. It was comforting each night to sleep in a comfortable bed and get some much-needed rest.

We continued to walk through a tunnel bridge with traffic passing over us, and when we came around the corner, we could hear music in the near distance. Through the trees, we could see a family having a picnic, playing guitars and passionately singing songs in Spanish. It was a treat to observe as we strolled by. It was as if we were being serenaded.

It reminded me of an earlier day when we met two Irish fellows walking in front of us singing away. I had decided each night to journal our days. On Day 8 our goal was to reach Los Arcos. This is where we caught up to our Irish friends, and as we passed them, I mentioned that Moira and I were both of Irish and British descent. They had lovely voices as they sang, and later said they would forgive us for our British heritage! Moira and I laughed. I told them my mom used to rock me on her lap when I was a little girl and sing "Oh Danny Boy," an old Irish folk tune.

Yes, they recalled that classic tune. The talented Senan started belting out "It's a long way to Tipperary," another familiar song

Moira and I remembered as kids. Senan told us while we walked with them how that song came about. It's the story of a young man who left his girl to go into the army, and he wrote it thinking of her while he was in combat. It was another famous British song popular amongst soldiers in the First World War and is remembered as a song of that war. As our Camino trek continued, our paths would cross again. Near the end of our journey, Senan from Ireland sang us a song he wrote about his journey when he was doing the Camino walk back in July 2013. He gave me permission to put it in my story and I loved his Irish lilt (accent) as he sang passionately outside a café in Burgos to a few of us pilgrims. He also sang the song my mom used to sing to me, "Oh Danny Boy." Senan had done 'The Way' 6 times, and in his email, he told me he sang every step of the way.

Senan's song Youtube.com at https://youtu.be/rsb992XdwwM. Buen Camino

Senan standing in front of us singing "Buen Camino"

Date: 19 July 2015 at 10:31:17 IST

Subject: BUEN CAMINO

BUEN CAMINO

AIR: Cockles and Mussels
(Low & Slow)

Chorus
Buen Camino
Buen Camino
Buen Camino
To Santiago.

Alternate Chorus
Santiago
Santiago
Santiago
Buen Camino

In faraway Spain, 'cross
mountains and plains,
I set on the route to Santiago,
For hundreds of years, midst
blood, sweat and tears,
With amigos and pilgrims a-
walkin' we'll go.

Chorus

So from St. Jean we pondered

Indeed, it's no wonder,
For centuries peregrinos ov'r
mountains did go
Across plains and valleys, with
back-packs and Sally's
All heading off to Santiago.

Chorus.

They've come from near and far
a-following His star,
Like shepherds a-wandering
like long, long ago,
Mind tossing and pondering,
soul searching and craving,
A-loving and sharing while
westwards we go.

Chorus

So I now say ' goodbye', with a
tear in my eye,
For homeward tomorrow, alas, I
must go,
For the great walk is ending,
but now I am singing,
For its then I'll begin my real
Camino.

Senan Lillis

Leon, N Spain 28th June 2013.

VIANA

Our next expedition on Day 10 was one I was so looking forward to. Leaving Los Arcos, we were heading to Viana where my friends from Canada were running the café called "The Pilgrims Oasis." The morning before we started our jaunt I sent my friend Sherry a text from the hotel telling her we would be walking to Viana and for them to look out for Debbie who would be arriving on the bus before us.

On the walk to Viana, we learned it would be much harder than it looked on a map. The high point of the day would be 600 meters of ups and downs of hilly terrain. I learned that Viana historically was built on a Roman settlement and in 1912, eight villages came together to create the town.

As we walked through scrubby gravel roads that wound up and down through the valley we saw many small ruins along the way. We passed by acres and acres of vineyards and olive trees planted back in Roman days. The Renaissance villages we passed along the way reminded me of ancient days long ago, with tall towers and the big black metal church bells clanging in the distance. Moira and I walked and finally arrived in the narrow streets of Viana.

I was in awe as I admired the majestic church of Santa Maria on the main street of pretty Viana. Built in the 12th century, the Gothic architect sculpted details displaying Renaissance history. It truly was a stunning masterpiece of yesteryear along the Camino Way. Viana is the last town on the Pilgrims' Way to Santiago in the Navarre region of northern Spain.

It was a really emotional moment for me as Moira and I found our way into beautiful Viana, walking past the little shops, as many of the locals sat at tables out for an early afternoon latte or lunch. We soon saw the sign "Pilgrims' Oasis," and wandered into the quaint café where we were welcomed with hugs and tears and smiles on Wes and Sherry's faces.

Wes prepared a wonderful cold foot bath with Epson salts for me, while Sherry helped Moira with her foot bath. Sherry shared that earlier she had stepped outside to see Debbie hobbling down the street and invited her into the café. We found out that our hotel was on the same block. To see familiar friends again, pausing to enjoy the serenity of the atmosphere in the cafe, and then to enjoy a cup of herbal tea and catch up, made this day of walking all worthwhile.

The next day we joined up with Patty from California who had also hurt her leg.

Wes and Sherry took the four of us out for a break to enjoy sites of the medieval towns and they set up a wine tour in the cellar of an ancient Basque fortress. There we watched an informative video of the crushing of the grapes. The season for the grape harvest was just days away and many locals would be a part of this celebration. We were sorry to miss it, but we had to continue on to our next destination. It would have been so much fun to join the townspeople in a huge barrel, stomping on grapes with our feet.

We made our way down the narrow stairs to the cellar to see the big, French oak and barrels where the wines were kept to age. We learned much about the history and influence and importance of the La Rioja wine-producing regions and culture of that time.

It was like a breath of fresh air to rest, enjoy the sites and do something completely different as we strolled past the ancient fountains, bakeries and tapas in the narrow streets. Wes navigated their little car safely within inches of passing other cars through the tiny alleyways as we continued to explore the loveliness of the little shops, ancient ruins, churches, and lookout points over the region. Later in the day, Wes and Sherry drove us to our next pit stop in Logrono.

Sherry, Wes, and me

Hope Nugget: Friendships and a cold foot bath bring solace to the soul.

Strolled into the Beautiful town of Viana

Outside Viana Spanish church bell

Outside a Viana lookout

Viana Architecture

Bird's Nest

Ancient Spanish Holy Water Basin

Love the Spanish Wood Doors

Three Girls at the Viana Courtyard Fountain

RAFAEL

Leaving Logrono, we headed out to Navarrete. Again, we left in the early morning to beat the heat of the day. We were advised to stock up on our water supply as there were no places along the way with fountains to fill up our water bottles. It would be 3 hours of walking through deserted landscapes before we would reach a town again. When we left Logrono, it seemed to take forever to get out of that city, but soon we made good progress.

The day I met Rafael from San Juan Puerto Rico was meant to be. I would call it one of those divine appointments in life. Moira and I were walking through a wooded park most of the morning with lovely tall trees everywhere on either side of the walking path.

We passed pilgrims along the way politely greeting them with our usual "Buen Camino," meaning "good road" or "good path," and carried on. It was another beautiful morning with the locals out jogging and walking along the way. A tall young man in his mid-forties kept passing me and then I would pass him. Eventually, we left the park and headed into the rugged terrain ahead. He was carrying a typical backpack with the familiar shell tied to his strap, and he was wearing sunglasses. He had long, dark, curly shoulder-length hair, and he reminded me of an artist or musician. Moira was enjoying her quiet time walking ahead of me. Rafael and I continued our journey together for the next couple of hours sharing life stories. I had been to San Juan (Saint John) the capital city, and he was surprised I knew of certain places that were very familiar to him in the cobblestoned older part of that town.

Puerto Rico is an American colony surrounded by beautiful beaches and Spanish colonial buildings dating back to the 1500's. My friend could speak fluent Spanish as he was born and raised in Puerto Rico.

The usual question was, "Why would you want to walk across Northern Spain?"

Rafael's story was unique because his younger brother, with whom he was really close, had been killed in a car accident some years back. Rafael had also recently broken up with a woman he was dating and was grieving the loss of both relationships in his life. We both understood grief, and I was able to share my own story with him. After a few hours of walking and chatting, we really connected.

I will never forget a really special moment we shared as we trekked along in the middle of nowhere. I mentioned to him that Bert had produced five albums over the years. Rafael pulled out his cell phone and asked me if his songs were on Spotify. I said, "I don't know," and he tapped Bert's full name into his Spotify list. We continued walking and out of the blue a song from Bert's "Seven Songs" CD "Look To You" began to play.

Can you imagine picturing this moment on a scorching, hot day on a rugged trail, when all of a sudden my husband's song begins playing in Spain. It felt like the title of the song, in that unusual moment, was appropriate. Unlike anything else I was expecting on this journey, there I was, listening to one of Bert's songs and sharing it with someone walking the same path as myself. Rafael put his ear-buds in his ears to listen to the album as we carried on along the way. I smiled to myself and thought what a special moment this was, sharing wonderful memories and songs with Rafael.

I eventually caught up with Moira to make our way through another town and then go on to our next haven to rest our sore feet. A few days later, I bumped into Rafael again, and this time he was not wearing his sunglasses. I have to say he had the most beautiful tender eyes that drew you into the softness of his heart. There was something really sweet, a boyishness reflecting a kind heart, about his demeanour. I am sure he has melted a few hearts over the years.

Included in our lodging each night was a
Pilgrim's dinner that included three starters to
choose from (soup, salad, fish) three mains
(fish, meat, potatoes and bread) and three
desserts (cheesecake, crème brulée, or ice
cream.) Rafael was staying in a nice hostel
near our hotel, so he invited us three girls to
come and have supper with him that night in a
very busy café on the upper level of the hostel.

As dinner was winding down amongst
some great conversations, I suddenly found
myself asking him if I could pray for him for
the things with which he was struggling.
Without missing a beat he said "Yes." He was
sitting across the table from me. I reached
over and took his hands in mine and prayed
out loud for him. I could sense a real peace
surrounding him, and I knew the Holy Spirit
was ministering in a special way, bringing
healing to his fractured heart. When I finished
praying he opened his eyes gently, took a
moment, and smiled so sweetly and thanked
me. I could tell something significant had
taken place in those few moments. There was
a peace lingering in the atmosphere. It felt as
though I heard the Lord whisper that Rafael
was loved and my prayer was a remarkable
seed being deposited into his life to give him a
hope and a future.

Hope Nugget: A kind word in season
soothes a longing heart.

LOOK TO YOU

In the quiet of the dawn, You're the one I
hope for
If I awake before You come, I will not give up
I will look to You in whatever comes my way
I will yield to You 'cause You are the only
way.

I throw away the things I've known
Throw away the lies again
Taking down the ways of old
Now it's Your love that leads me home.

Chorus:
Though the feelings run so strong
Still, by faith, I know I belong
Still, Your love leads me along
You're the song within my heart

Many times I've seen the light
That shines above my head
It's then I know that You're the way I'm
headed for
I will look to You in whatever comes my way
I will yield to You 'cause You are the only
way.

Bert Petkau Seven Songs CD
2011

LOST AND FOUND

Moira and I then trudged along close to the highway as trucks sped by honking with encouragement. They all knew we were pilgrims walking along the narrow gravel path close to the N120. The air was filled with gas fumes in the hot sun as we quickly strolled through cornfields and farmlands into one of many small villages en route today. We knew that on our 24 km jaunt there would be plenty of places to refuel with water and food.

In the early morning, we stopped to buy a latte and rested for a few minutes before we headed out again to Najera. Then we grabbed our packs and stepped outside to head out "On the Road Again." No pun intended; I think this is the name of a Willie Nelson song!

Leaving a quaint village, we walked down the hill and turned left onto another dusty road. We walked for a few hours and came across a familiar Camino marking that was usually highlighted with a yellow arrow and a scallop shell. These painted symbols were highlighted throughout the whole Camino way to help pilgrims stay on track. We found them on walls in small towns, tiles, rocks, bridges, and sidewalks. They were well marked out so it would make it hard to get lost along the way.

What was unusual about this marking was that the arrow was painted blue instead of yellow and it threw us off, so we were not sure whether to go left or right at the fork in the road. We should have taken a minute to think it through before proceeding. Instead, we ignored the blue arrow and wandered along the path for some time. It was another scorching hot day, and the further we walked we somehow knew we were off the beaten path. As we rambled through a vineyard, we couldn't see any other travellers coming or going either way. We decided to stop by a tree for some shade and Moira pulled out her guide book to see how far off we were.

All of a sudden out of nowhere, an angel appeared in the form of Lee from South Korea. We shared our dilemma with him and he pulled out his cell phone with GPS displaying distance, time and a compass in place. We could see a town way off in the distance but figured it was probably not our final destination for the day. Lee had started his own walk not long after us in St. Jean Pied in France. He had taken two months off from his job, and he had been walking day and night. He had a headlight for night walks, and he said it was peaceful and beautiful walking under the stars that guided him in the dark.

I soon found out he was the same age as one of my sons and physically very fit. He had trained in the army in Korea and could handle a lot. Lee and I walked together while Moira, steady and strong, strolled ahead of us. He decided to trek this road because his GPS showed it was something of a short cut to Najera, the next stop for the three of us. As we shared our life stories, I couldn't believe it when he told me he was a structural engineer in Seoul, South Korea. We both were surprised when I told him I also worked in administration for an engineering firm.

I had some business cards in my backpack and mentioned, as we walked, that our company was looking for fresh faces to come and work at our firms. We were interested in hiring civil and structural engineers. He was thrilled to hear that and said he would love to come to Vancouver one day and perhaps work there or in the area. You never know where life will take you!

With the help of Lee's GPS we continued to walk and the town we assumed was our next destination was not where we were to rest our weary feet. We walked around the village rather than go through it as we were tired, hot, and thirsty. We pushed through and marched forward to our next place of rest. It was a long day, but we realized how blessed we were to have our Camino angel, Lee, to steer us to our next stop. Without him, who knows where we would have ended up. Lee's hostel was in the same town as ours, and he put the address of our inn into his phone and walked us directly to the front door. With tears of joy, we thanked him for rescuing us along the way. I did give him one of my business cards. This fine young man was truly an angel who came out of nowhere to lead us to safety to our hotel.

In the book of Hebrews 13:2 ESV it says: *do not neglect to show hospitality to strangers, for thereby some have entertained angels unawares.*

I think back to that day and still remember us standing by the one and only tree for shade trying to figure out our dilemma when Lee came around the corner. We were very grateful.

Puenta de Najera Hostel

Hope Nugget: Angels are on assignment when we ask and pray.

Early morning latte

Camino Marker and Arrow Keeps us on Track

FREE TO RUN

I hear Your whisper in the morning
I feel You softly in the night
Your words so wise go beyond reason
Your words are strong and I know it's right.

Chorus:
Ooh ooh ooh ooh, You surround me
Ooh ooh ooh ooh, You'll never leave me
Oooh ooh ooh ooh, You surround me.

Distant shadows will not find me
Broken dreams will see the day
Faded lights no longer hide me
'Cause in Your love I see the way.

Bridge:
Though those dark clouds do surround me
They rise beneath the sun
And when I feel the wind against me
I feel free to run.

Bert Petkau Seven Songs CD
2011

TURNING THE CORNER OF OUR TRIP

Moira wanted to stay and keep Debbie company, so I ended up walking with Lucy, my new friend from England, to Santa Domingo de la Calzada. It was a 20 km walk. I was grateful for Lucy's company as we headed through huge cereal fields and mile-high stacked haystacks of this clearly agricultural region. This was one of the best days of our expedition, with a few clouds in the sky and the refreshment of a cool breeze after all the treacherous hot days we had overcome. The gentle wind upon our faces made this trek so much easier.

We reached the village of Azofra where Lucy and I sat down to have lunch and a rest. We chatted with other pilgrims before we carried on. Lucy had wifi on her cell, so we checked out our route, to find we had a choice of two different routes to reach our next destination. We could go on the noisier, less scenic route along the highway, adding 3 km in total to San Domingo or we could climb the hill up towards Ciruena and then go back down over railroad tracks into Santa Domingo.

We decided, because of the weather, to go up the hill. Thus we avoided three kilometers. The walk didn't seem to be difficult because of the slight wind and coolness of the day. I remember the photos I took at the crest of the hill with those on bikes riding the Camino and the many others walking along the way with us.

We eventually travelled on a downward slope, taking care to place our feet amongst the loose rocks and with delight, we strolled into our next destination earlier than we had expected, less tired, and filled with anticipation to carry on. Lucy Googled my hotel to find out where I was staying, and she found her Albergue (hostel) four minutes away.

I went in to get my Camino passport stamped and then met up with Moira for a little tour of the town amongst the locals in Santa Domingo. We stepped into a little boutique to check out the fashions and sales of the day. Later we met up with Debbie to enjoy our Pilgrims' dinner. It was kind of a nice change to be served in the quiet café as the three of us had the little restaurant to ourselves.

Lucy and I stopping for a latte

Biking the Camino

Pilgrims on the path

The Road Less Travelled

BUTTERFLIES

Along the Camino, right from the start of our journey, I would often see butterflies. Brilliant coloured varieties of purple, orange, yellow, red, and blue. Every few days as we sauntered amongst the grassy shrubs, one or two would appear beside me or in front of me as if to inspire and motivate me to continue on. They would flutter up and down and around me as if to say, "This is the way to go and you can do it."

Moira would notice them as well and say, "Teresa there is your Camino friend again rooting you on" and she would say, "Bert is watching over you and cheering you on this trek."

I would smile and think, just like out-of-the-blue Lee, the butterflies were my little angels watching over us as we trekked putting one foot in front of the other. Especially on those scorching hot days and where there was not much shade to be found.

While I was walking along, I was reflecting upon my life and all the changes I have experienced over the past four years. I thought of butterflies and the whole process they go through. There are 4 different stages that occur from egg to larva in a butterfly's life cycle. Chrysalis is a 10 to14 day cycle where a hard shell is spun by a caterpillar in which growth and transformation takes place. The caterpillar then spins a cocoon usually in the warmth of the summer. It can take up to two weeks for the process to complete and eventually, at the end of the procedure, a beautiful butterfly emerges.

I was thinking of all the stages and activity that take place for the caterpillar and all the undertakings that have gone on in my life. Though it wasn't easy, I was realizing that when I do let go completely, my metamorphosis or my transformation is not so difficult when I am dependant on God. Most vital is for us to trust that He is taking care of us in each one of our destinies and for us to leave things in His hands to mold and shape. I was thinking that as I am in the cocooning process, it is a safe place where my growth is taking place. It takes time and patience as we, like the caterpillar, in the cycle of our lives eventually burst forth to become the beautiful butterfly, a renewed child of God. A son or a daughter. Don't you find in each season or chapter of our lives this process seems to repeat itself?

Trust in the Lord with all of your heart, and do not lean on your own understanding. In all your ways acknowledge him, and he will make straight your paths. Proverbs 3:5-6 ESV.

As we were traipsing along the path, I thought back to a special time in July 2018. That's when a special event took place in my home town of Abbotsford, B.C., Canada. That summer a group of women, including myself, gathered together in a beautiful private garden, one warm Saturday morning, to honour a friend who had just passed away because of brain cancer. She was a special lady and had overcome much in her life. My friend Joanne and I would go regularly to hospice and pray for her and encourage her. Shortly before her passing one Sunday afternoon, we helped Laura into her wheelchair and took her outside to get some fresh air. She would comment, "Oh I love the air and look at the beautiful flowers in the garden." We would wheel her chair beside the little stream that ran through the garden so she could listen to the soothing sound of the water. She asked us for a favour that after her passing we would come back to this special place and have a little memorial for her with a small group of her girlfriends. She asked us to remember her after her regular celebration of life with her family. Tears welling up in our eyes we said, "Of course, Laura we will."

Joanne has a video of her making that request, and I promised I would say the prayer when we would gather again in honour of her life. I have tears in my eyes right now just thinking of that special day with Laura. I seemed to have come into her life for a reason, and she was forever grateful to me, sharing with me how Bert had hired her son on one of his jobs when he was a young teenager.

Bert graciously took him under his wing and put up with some of his teenage shenanigans. On my regular Sunday visits to hospice that summer, she told me Bert was one of the kindest men she ever knew and she really admired him. What a small world it is when people come and go in our lives, all for a greater purpose.

That Saturday morning as we had promised, nine girls who knew Laura gathered at that garden to honour her after she passed. We laughed and cried sharing stories about her, remembering her with fondness on that beautiful summer morning. We later went to "Tanglebank Gardens" where the hospice in our city was having a real butterfly release to give tribute to friends and loved ones who had gone on. We each held little tiny boxes with real butterflies inside and opened the lids slowly careful not to touch the butterfly wings. As the warmth of the sun touched each butterfly, it lifted up into the air and danced away into freedom. Some of our local newspaper reporters were on hand for the event, taking photos. Unknown to me one of the cameras zoomed in on me as I cautiously released my butterfly and I ended up in our local Abbotsford News paper that week.

One of the special ladies there that day was my new friend Jane Welch. In the Spring of 2018, she had come to the signing ceremony at the release of my first book, *A Fountain of Hope*. And now here she was at Tanglebank with Connie Sales, Joanne Field and some others I knew when I was first married.

Jane and I had this instant connection, like we were kindred spirits, yet we hardly knew each other. We met for coffee a few times later in the year, and we were amazed by the many friends we had in common. The two of us could spend hours together talking about anything over a hot cup of tea and leave like it was yesterday to catch up all over again. Friendships with women are very special as you move forward, living life. New friendships are formed and sometimes old ones can come and go as I have experienced over the years.

As I trekked along on some of those hot days in Spain for miles and miles, with little butterflies fluttering around me, I would think of Jane and the special moments we have shared in life. And we know there are more to come. She is a joyful, wise woman, and I am glad to call her friend.

In the Fall of 2018, I purchased my friend Joanne's home because she and her husband were moving up to northern BC to be with their family. My son-in-law Dennis did an amazing four-month renovation to my new place, and it turned out spectacular. In early May of 2019, I had a going-away tea for Joanne and the butterfly girls, as I call them. All of them except one came to celebrate Joanne's move and the next chapter of her life.

Jane, Terry, Connie, Christine, Alicia, Heather have been coffee friends for years. These ladies had all been in Joanne's place before I bought and renovated it. It was a special day as we celebrated my new home and the continuation of what God had in store for Joanne as well. Jane I love the butterfly magnet you gave me for my screen door that day.

I thought of my butterfly friends dancing amongst the brush, rooting for me in the scrubby grass hedges on many dusty roads in Spain.

Hope Nugget: Friendships with other women are like butterflies gracious and joyous.

Joyce's Butterfly

My Butterfly Friend

Butterfly Picture of Jane and the Girls in Abbotsford

Teresa's Newspaper Picture

ME TO YOU

If I got something to give
To give to you, If I've got something to sing

I'll sing to you
I'll sing to you
I'll sing to you

I won't hold nothing back
Not a thing from you.
And if I want someone to think about
I'll think of you

And if my mind starts to wander
It's still to you
It's still to you
It's still to you
In everything I do it's still to you

Oh oh oh oh, you you you Oh oh oh oh you
you you

And if there's someone to believe in
That will make it true
You will see me break through from the
shadows
From me to you From me to you
From me to you

               Bert Petkau Lights & Oceans
               CD 2014

ALMOST THERE

Moira and I were up and ready to go at 8 am to have breakfast and leave our suitcases in the lobby as we prepared ourselves to head out on our 23 km trek to Belorado. We crossed the bridge over the River Oja amongst gravel footpaths near the freeway N120. Our early morning walk took us to our first uphill climb that was steep but not very long. My heart was always beating a mile a minute on those inclines, and once I reached the top, I stopped to catch my breath.

Our first village of many to enter that day was Granon. It was the last village that we would pass through in the state of La Rioja. We once again came across some familiar faces on our Camino walk. We met Frank and Aileen from Niagara Falls Ontario, Patty from California and an older French couple that stayed at some of the same hotels as we did. We stopped for our morning lattes, catching up about our adventures and grateful we would be walking in weather that was cool for most of the day.

Moira and I walked over to the parish church of San Juan Bautista that dates back to the 14th century in Granon. We also walked into another beautiful little church that morning to get our passports stamped.

Simultaneously we sat down to rest in the quietness. I knelt on the pew, and my mind went back in time, flooding me with memories of my Catholic background of similar pews in the late 1960's. We took time to pray, reflect, and enjoy God's peace in the surroundings of candles lit.

We could see that the ornate, embellished carvings on the walls and the architecture inside had been mastered over time by handcrafted guilders. We sat in silence resting in the peace that only God can provide. Leaving the pretty little church, we walked amongst many acres of farmlands and wheat fields with Patty from California. She had joined us on our day off in Vianna as we visited with Wes and Sherry. We walked awhile sharing our stories, and I found out that Patty lived outside the Sierra Nevada mountains in Nevada. She had lost her son, a young paratrooper, in battle, and she was walking her own journey in honour of him.

She had tears in her eyes, as she dealt with her own personal pain and grief, as we walked side-by-side. I was filled with compassion for her loss. We exchanged our own personnel stories, grateful we could comfort one another and understand the pain we both had experienced. Moira and I walked her to her hostel 8 km away before we made our way to the cutest hotel in Belorado Casa Rural Vereancho.

In the late afternoon we strolled through the town, wandering into the main plaza where locals gathered for a drink. We met Lucy and others to share about our adventures of the day, sipping refreshments and relaxing.

Praying

Cutest Room

Benchmark Camino Sign

BELARADO TO
ATAPUERCA

September 26, 2018, Lucy and I met up in the early morning. We wanted to beat the sun and get an early start, knowing we had quite a hike ahead of us. I mentally prepared myself to climb one of the longest and most difficult mountains called the Montes de Oca (1,150 metres in height). We walked in the sun that morning until we came to the truck-stop town of Villafranca Montes de Oca for a rest and a latte.

I reflected, remembering that here, if you sat down to rest and not purchase something, the host behind the truck-stop trailer would yell something in Spanish at you while waving their hands in disgust. The couple watched like hawks to see who occupied their white plastic chairs, as they were aware there was no food or water for miles after this stop. I got up and purchased another bottle of water and took off my shoes and socks to rest my achy feet in the shade. Not far from the food trailer, we made our way turning left to a steep climb into the Montes de Oca. The sharp incline had us stopping along the way, grateful for the shaded trees to catch our breath along the path. Lucy and I walked into a forest with pine and oak trees on either side, that seemed to go on forever. However, the beauty of the trees covered a quiet walk where we were shaded and enjoyed the tranquility on this pathway.

We found our way to the small village of San Juan de Ortega, and I walked into the ancient church to take a photo of an antique Spanish bible laying on a table. Its tattered pages told the familiar story of 2000 years ago, written in Spanish proclaiming the scriptures Genesis to Revelations. The oversized bell in the steeple outside was something to behold. Lucy and I left the charm and history for another 6 km walk to Atapeurca. Eventually, we made our way down a ragged, rocky hill filled with rocks and more rocks that led us eventually into San Juan de Ortega.

Hope Nugget: Grateful for God providing a walking partner when I needed one.

It was here I would bump into my friends Rafael from Puerto Rico and Lee from South Korea for the last time. I found them resting and having a drink outside a local café. Rafael noticed me finishing my trek for that day and called out my name. I walked over to say our final goodbyes, as he was heading on a train to Barcelona to visit a friend, and then back home to Puerto Rico. He again thanked me for the prayer and in Spanish style, gave me a kiss on each one of my cheeks. I gave Lee a hug, as I knew this was a short pit stop for him as

he was determined to finish 'the way' right
into Santiago de Compostela.

Church Bells

OUR LAST LEG OF THE
JOURNEY

On September 27th Moira and I got up early to walk our last hike together - a 22km walk to the city of Burgos.

We woke up early that morning and our host Rosa dropped us back onto the Camino path. The morning was misty with fog settling upon the farmlands. We climbed up another steep hill, the Sierra de Atapuerca, carefully placing our steps amongst the rocks that reminded me of cragged, white stones found in the ruins in Athens, Greece.

When we reached the summit, we came across the most beautiful scene. A huge, stately cross stood beside the path. With the sun rising amongst the early morning darkness accompanied by the moon in the distance, and a swirling mist lingering everywhere, it looked like angelic hosts filled the hilltop with silent peace.

I took off my backpack and crossed my arms to look up at the wonder of the cross not knowing Moira snapped a photo of me with the brilliant yellow-orange sun directly over my head.

It was one of those special shots where perfect timing in the moment becomes magical, a wonder.

Moira and I with the Cross at Sunrise

IN THE AMBER MORNING

In the amber morning as stars start to fade
The light shines through the shadows once
again
And right here under heaven. This side of the
veil
There's something more and it's rising higher

Hey hey hey, hey hey yeah
A spark starts the fire

The strong wind is blowing
I know it's coming there
It's in my heart I feel it everywhere

Can you feel the movement
Can you feel it coming strong
Can you feel the heart of one that's higher

Ooh – A spark starts the fire
Ooh – Love lift me higher

TAG
A spark starts the fire. A spark sets the flame
to glow
Love lift me higher. Love let it overflow.

Bert Petkau Seven Songs CD
2011

We continued on the Camino path, walking through two more villages called Ages and Atapuerca. We stopped for a latte in the latter village as a Bob Dylan song played inside the café. The song brought the familiarity of North America to the sweetness of the Spanish culture we were enjoying. After leaving the village, we discovered we could take one of two routes to eventually reach the city of Burgos. We decided to cross the motorway and ended up walking many miles around what seemed to be an airport strip.

The hot sun was upon us again as we trudged along the river route eventually reaching the outskirts of a beautiful park on the edge of the well-established city of Burgos.

Burgos

The river Arlanzon meandered along as we walked for what seemed forever through the Paseo del Espolon Park to our final destination into the city of Burgos. We made our way across the bridge into the hustle and bustle of cars rushing by, shoppers everywhere looking for the best in fashions and the noise of crowds filling streets in the buzzing commerce section of Burgos.

Moira and I were pretty spent, but we stopped by a shoe store to window shop for a minute and admire the latest in Spanish fashion. I've heard that in North America it takes a year or so for us to catch up to the latest styles and fashions of Europe.

Wandering through the streets, we soon found our final hotel nestled amongst a great shopping area. It was truly surreal for me when we walked into the hotel to get my last stamp for my Camino passport and tears welled up in my eyes.

It was dream-like knowing that I had accomplished what I set out to do on this journey and walked my race well. Soon we would be in Madrid to fly back to the familiarity of home. I told Moira I needed some time to process by myself and went up to my room to take a warm shower and rest my feet. The warmth of the clean water and the pulsating shower head as the water ran down me felt heavenly. Refreshed I sat on my bed journaling and reflected upon the journey I had just finished. It was exhilarating and yet unreal in that moment as a flood of emotions washed over me. I remembered facing the unknown three weeks beforehand and the ups and downs of this huge venture now triumphantly finished. I had trekked 300 km across a beautiful country that echoed the history of thousands of other pilgrims walking the same path. It was unbelievable to think about all of the steps we had taken in less than three weeks and to think we were getting on a plane to fly home soon.

In the afternoon I left the hotel and went for a walk around the shopping district of Burgos to take in some of the sites and culture. That evening Moira remembered I was looking for a wooden cross that I could bring with me to put in my new home. My son-in-law was working evenings every day renovating while I was away. Moira surprised me and took me into a store that had all kinds of Catholic items like rosary beads, statues of Mary and other saints with all of the price tags written in Spanish. It brought back memories again of my Catholic childhood. We went up to the lady behind the counter who spoke no English. Moira got her attention and typed some words on her phone to ask that I was looking for a simple wood cross without Jesus on it. She seemed to understand and with enthusiasm went to the back of her shop and came out with a simple piece of wood in the shape of a cross. What a special memento! I love it and it hangs on the wall in my office with the photo of the sun and the cross enlarged on my wall.

We walked down the street back to the store we came across earlier that afternoon and decided to treat ourselves to a pair of stylish boots for me and shoes for Moira. We were delighted our trekking treads were no longer needed.

When I wear those ankle boots from Spain at home or to work, it is a sweet reminder of all the footprints I left along the Camino way.

Last Fall when I got back from our trek I was able to make a video of my journey with all the photo stops along the way, starting in the Pyrenees Mountains bordering France and finishing in Burgos in Northern Spain. The video is cued to the song *I would walk 500 miles* by the musical group The Proclaimers.

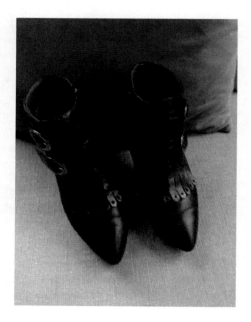

These Boots Were Made for Walking...

Burgos cathedral Arco de Santa Maria

The Three Amigos Heading Home

Airport Starbucks

CYPRUS

On Wednesday October 9th I flew from Vancouver to London England and then onto Larnaka Cyprus to visit my good friends Chris and Rosalee Barton. The two long flights were worth the travels as I immersed myself in the warmth of the sun and the many dips in the Mediterranean Sea.

Cyprus is a country divided into two areas with the Cypriot Greeks in the south and a legal border that separates the occupied Turkish Cypriots in the North. Many Cypriot Greeks fled from the north in 1974 when a Turkish invasion happened. The southern part of the island is predominantly Greek with a large Russian presence in the city of Nicosia.

My friends drove me to the Limassol Salt Lakes that fill with water in the winter months. These lakes are protected heritage sites where poised flamingos migrate to Larnaka the end of November from Africa. They come to rest and to eat the algae from the surrounding lakes. Thousands upon thousands of these beautiful wading birds line the shores flying from one of the three salt lakes to find a resting spot for winter. It was the end of October and they had come earlier this year to migrate and it was a treat to see them so eloquently standing like ballerinas in the shallow salt shoreline. When they lift their wings there is a beautiful pink undercoat that changes color because of the algae they ingest.

In Larnaka where I was staying I would walk down to the beautiful beach each day and stroll along the promenade. It is a popular tourist destination and Larnaka is the capital city of Cyprus. Not far from the shops and cafes is the beautiful 9th century Church of Saint Lazarus. It belongs to the Church of Cyprus, a Greek Orthodox Church many of them scattered through the southern part of the island. This church lies over the tomb of the saint known as Lazarus a familiar miracle where Jesus raises him from the dead. The miraculous story is found in the bible in the book of John. After the Resurrection of Christ Lazarus was forced to flee Judea and he came to Cyprus. He was ordained as Bishop of Kition by the apostles Barnabas and Paul and lived in the town of Larnaka. He lived there for thirty years and after his second death was buried in Larnaka. The church of Agios Lazaros is the church that was built over his tomb.

Something I marveled at in Cyprus was the luscious pomegranates, oranges, lemons, grapes, avocados and other fresh fruits that were huge in size and in abundance. Inexpensive vegetables and other fruits lined the stalls at local vendors' markets and grocery stores. Fresh tins of olive oil produced in Cyprus, olives, spices, pickles were in abundance especially in the Turkish markets in the north. I brought home tins of olive oil for my pantry and gifts for my friends and family. I love the taste of fresh olive oil, olives, feta cheese, cucumbers and cherry tomatoes topped with fresh basil and oregano spices from Cyprus makes for an enjoyable Greek salad.

A few days near the end of my two week stay with Chris and Rosalie, we drove up to the East

of Cyprus crossing the Turkish border to visit
the beautiful ruins of Salamis. Many years ago
it was the capital city of Cyprus in 1100 B.C.
Over the centuries the Persians, Jews,
Christians, Greeks and Arabs once occupied this
once bustling port city. I love the marble pillars
still standing and the colorful unique patterned
tiles that lined the weathered paths amongst
the dirt and grit. There was also a beautiful
beach near this heritage site where many were
snorkeling the blue green waters of the
Mediterranean Sea.

It was an eye opener to see the different ways
of life in the North compared to the South of
Cyprus. The country of Turkey is the only
country in the world that recognizes the Turkish
Cypriots who occupy the land in Northern
Cyprus. We made our way up to Varosha in
Famagusta on the east coast of Cyprus. This is
where in 1974 40,000 Greek Cypriots were
attacked by Turkish troops and fled from their
homes with only the clothes on their backs to
southern Cyprus. They lost their homes and
belongings and never went back. This was once
a luxurious resort city now fenced off by barb

wire and heavily guarded by Turkish military. It has been a ghost town ever since. We drove around to take a look and all I could see was dilapidated high rises, stores, gas stations, restaurants, a community frozen in time now empty a town where vines grow over buildings, rust and heartache are memories of a once thriving town. Families went back to collect their belongings but it was too dangerous to stay. It was a mix of eeriness and sadness viewing from the windows of our vehicle as I thought of the pain of those involved more than forty years ago.

On a good note Cyprus is filled with beauty, culture, delicious foods, restaurants, history and many different cultures. I experienced wonderful Lebanese food one night – Baba Ghanouge roasted eggplant, hummus and falafels, (chickpea bean patties with various Mediterranean spices) and lots of pita bread. The presence of the Greek Orthodox churches throughout southern Cyprus leaves you with a reverence for God and the freedoms the Greeks enjoy.

One awesome experience that happened to me that I was not expecting was when I arrived into Larnaka on my first night. My friends picked me up from the airport and I was aware they were also expecting another friend arriving the same day from Northern Ireland for a few days. They arranged with a friend of theirs for me to stay two days with her as their house was full and I was fine with that. I had never met Bobbi before when I was dropped off at her place in the wee hours of the morning when my flight arrived in Larnaka. She welcomed me with open arms and I slept well from my long day of travels and set my alarm to Cyprus time. The next morning over coffee we spent time getting to know each other. We hit it off right away. She was curious about my writing and shared with me how she always wanted to write a book. I happened to bring a few copies of "A Fountain of Hope" and pulled one from my backpack and gave it to her. Bobbi was also an avid walker and loved to do long walks around Larnaka. I told her about the second story I just finished writing about my travel adventures and mostly about my walk across northern

Spain and my pilgrimage of the Camino. Her eyes lit up as I shared my story and she was intrigued. We spent the next two days sharing our life stories and how we both liked to travel. We had a strong connection and on the last day of my Cyprus stay we went out for coffee. Somehow on that last day I felt we were going to go back to Spain together and do some more walking, another portion of the Camino de Santiago. Sure enough that is the plan and we are both excited to continue this new adventure for her as well a continued trek for me. I believe God had an unknown surprise for me, more than a place for me to stay for a few nights in Larnaka. I gained a new friend

and walking partner to finish what I started on the Camino and we will walk together into Santiago de Compostela to receive our certificates of completion at the Cathedral de Santiago de Compostela where Saint James tomb rests. I often wondered if I would ever go back and now I am. How exciting!

Ninth Century Church of St. Lazarus – Lazarus' Tomb

Ruins of Salamis

Capital City Larnaka Cyprus

Luscious Grapes

Cypriot Greek Southern Cyprus

Southern Cyprus

Market Northern Cyprus

Salamis Northern Cyprus

Market Place

Northern Cyprus

FACING OUR MOUNTAINS

Somehow through this story I wanted to share some of my experiences that have shaped me to be who I am today and to offer you the reader the thought that whatever we go through in life, especially the challenges we all face day to day, are what God uses to strengthen us, and bring hope to encourage others. The mountain-top experiences of my life have been wonderful. We need to have them to appreciate our accomplishments and to have those joyous times. I have found that it is in some of the lowest points of my despair, experiencing grief and hopelessness, that I have found the faith to look upward. It is in those most unexpected moments that I see God in His mercy meet me, to have faith and understand that He is in all of our life trials.

It may be the tiniest of seeds but a mustard seed, barely visible to the eye, yet our Heavenly Father uses it in His word as an object of faith. Though the seed is so tiny, it matters. When I release my faith and believe God is right there to intervene and give me the strength to climb my mountains, He helps me get through my struggles. I am learning to embrace my circumstances, trusting God to bring good out of them. My experiences teach me to rely more fully on Him rather than on my own ability. When I realized how independent I have become, in some ways and having to be, I see I must not be self-sufficient but continue to trust, let go and depend on God through intimacy and growth. It is in the surrender that the mustard seed so small moves mountains.

Right now I think of the time about six years ago in July, when Bert and I climbed up the backside of Mount Cheam in the Fraser Valley near where I reside. It took us about an hour to reach the top of the summit on a clear day. We looked over panoramic unobstructed views of Agassiz, Chilliwack and beyond Mt. Baker in Washington and east towards Hope, B.C.

The day we stood on top of the ridge, a glider went whizzing by above us, majestically gliding over the mountain top. We stood in awe, watching him pass by, waving to him and taking in the breathless beauty of creation around us. I have the joy of knowing each day as I drive to work, that ahead of me and staring back at me, is the sublime beauty of the white, snow-capped peak of Mount Cheam. I smile to myself knowing that the adventure of hiking that mountain carries special memories. As we face our own mountains in life, we can overcome them and reach the summit through Abba's help.

The Pinnacle of Mt. Cheam

SONS AND DAUGHTERS OF
THE MOST HIGH

Not in myself can I overcome challenges, but Jesus has the power to give us the kind of courage it takes to live our lives fearlessly. It is not allowing fear to call the shots in our lives and really believing we are His sons and daughters seated in heavenly places with Him. When we know in Him as our identity, we see from a different perspective. We understand we are His sons and daughters and can embrace and truly believe He lives inside each one of us that believe in Him.

People who know that their identity is in Christ are love-carriers and are not afraid to be vulnerable, free to be themselves and carry a hope that ignites freedom to others around them. I think of children, especially when they are young and innocent, who simply believe and have a trusting faith that things will work out in life. We need to be like children having peace, knowing with childlike trust that God is taking care of everything that concerns us. It is wonderful to know God's ardent love for us and that in every nanosecond of each day, our love flourishes when we long to please Him. He wants us to be our true authentic selves because each one of us has a destiny to fulfill.

With the quality of life I have been given, I find it important to understand the spiritual truths of the Bible I hold onto and to practice these truths daily in my life. It is in the day in and day out routines of life where we can make a difference in others' lives. What does that look like for you?

I love my job and the people with whom I work. The days have slipped by so quickly, and I now realize that I have been employed for three years. Even though the familiarity of the job has found a rhythm of its own for me, I still love my job and the people I get to work with. There are days it is so busy I feel satisfied yet exhausted by the time I leave the office.

For some who have worked in settings for years and years, drudging it, I would say it is how you approach each day that makes it rewarding even in the mundane day to day affairs. As we walk through the routines of our days, even when nothing special seems to be happening, there is an invisible thing occurring in the spirit when we are able to be faithful in the little things. God is working behind the scenes. There is a reward in the outcome of that obedience because we are trusting God and collaborating with Him to do things together through a merger of trust and love. I am thankful for the way my job came to me and for the perfect timing of how it all came together. I am grateful I get to do life with those I work with. I don't believe things happen for no reason. I'm sure I am there to make a difference. It is true that faith, hope and most of all love, have an effect on the lives of other people.

There are of course those days when challenges arise, and I am not always positive in the way I think about things. It is important to recognize the enemy in those difficult moments and not let him steal my peace.

It is not so much the task at hand, but what we do that is super important it is being sensitive to those around us and making a difference in their lives. God cares more about the people we are in contact with than the tasks we focus on. I am learning to step out and genuinely take an interest in whoever comes across my path. This may be at the coffee shop where I stop to pick up my latte in the mornings, being friendly to the staff, thanking them for taking the time to make my coffee and telling them to have a wonderful day as well. We have been given the power to change the atmosphere through God's love in us. I love the smiles that come across peoples faces and how they light up when we genuinely show that we care.

Beauty in Spain

Hope Nugget: **Bloom where your planted.**

CHOICES WE MAKE

It takes a measure of faith to believe
through adverse situations, that there is a
cloud with a silver lining somewhere along
the way. It is easy and understandable to want
to condemn ourselves and to give up when
things don't go the way we expect. Our
thoughts are so powerful that we can drift
through painful situations and listen to those
tapes that play in our minds, believing it's
alright to check out mentally or isolate
ourselves from people and the world around
us. It can become a downward spiral and even
lead to depression and mental illness. In my
own city, and the town where I am employed,
a 25-minute drive from my home, it saddens
me to see so many homeless people. As I
drive by in the mornings on my way to work,
there's sure to be someone pushing a buggy
full of belongings. Another one will be sitting
against a building, starring aimlessly. I work
in the downtown area of the business center in
an older part of the city. When I look out the
window from my desk, I see a lot of oppressed
and broken people wandering the streets,
passing by our building. Often times, they go
into the alleyway beside our building to do
drugs or hang out on our back porch. It breaks
my heart to see them and to hear them acting
out in outrageous ways. There are many days I

have to call security to have them come and remove these individuals. Life can be cruel. How did these people end up this way, so bruised and fractured? Each one of them is somebody's child, and each one has a story. I often cry out to God, asking Him how can I make a difference to help in some way.

My prayer for each one of them is that God would take them out of the darkness they find themselves in, and they would experience His mercy and forgiveness through Jesus Christ and the extravagant love He paid for each one of them by His shed blood. I realize it is a choice every day what decisions we make, good or bad, that affect the outcome of our lives.

Not too long ago on a Thursday morning, I drove to work as usual. There were many boxes of files lining the floor of our office that needed to go to our storage unit. Brian, one of the engineers, helped me load them into my vehicle, and I headed to the storage place not too far away from our office. Later that morning as I was returning to my work, I noticed the traffic lights were not working, so it was stop and go at each light. Barricades were placed across side streets close to where I am employed. When I walked into our office all the power was off, no phones were ringing, and none of the computers were working. What had happened was a warehouse just down the street from us burnt down and caused the hydro transformer to blow out. Sirens from police cars and fire trucks were going non-stop for several hours. I later found out that the unusual explosions from the fire were caused by highly flammable chemicals that were ignited by a drug lab and its toxins.

In the middle of the power outage, our fellow employees in the civil engineering department were having a "Lunch and Learn." This is where outside clients come in to give a presentation to promote the development of products for construction and engineering. The staff enjoyed Subway sandwiches while listening as the speakers shared about the new techniques they were offering.

After the meeting was finished, I helped to clean up the leftover food and wrapped the extra sandwiches in plastic wrap. Trusting that our power would turn on soon, I put the leftovers into our fridge. I left the office to go and do the daily banking down the street. I then headed to the city building department to drop off some drawings. On my way back it seemed to take forever to get through the street lights and the traffic was piling up in both lanes.

Earlier that afternoon, one of the engineers, Drew, had stopped by my desk to show me a photo he had just taken on his phone. He had just come back from his lunch, and he noticed a girl in her early twenties sitting in the back alley digging through the garbage bags. My heart was torn as I looked at the photo. Drew mentioned to me she was higher than a kite and in her own little world.

I found myself saying, "Would you come outside with me to give her a large Subway sandwich?"

"Of course."

We opened the back door and stepped outside into the alley. Walking towards her, I noticed she was filthy and her hair had not been combed in a while. She had no shoes on her feet and her dirty flip flops lay beside the garbage. We walked over to her and I said, "Honey would you like a sandwich?" She looked up at me sideways for a moment trying to focus. As she reached out to take the food, she thanked me and complimented me on the top I was wearing. I looked at her with compassion as tears welled up in my eyes, wishing I could do something more. I wanted to swoop her up and take her to a place of safety, hoping a morsel of nutrition could be of some help. Drew and I walked back into the office where the power was still out. I sat down at my desk in the silence, asking God to have mercy on the young woman and that somehow, through my little prayer, He in His grace would rescue her.

As children of God, we are called to be barrier-breakers in this world and to demonstrate His love in a way that would affect those around us each day. I think it takes facing my own fears and stepping outside my comfort zone to love even the unlovely. I think as I do this I will understand the true meaning of helping others that are hurting because love is Jesus living inside of me.

People who become love, don't care what others think of them, because they are so filled with love and compassion of the kind that Jesus demonstrated throughout the New Testament. They will do whatever it takes to reach hurting people.

I am growing on my journey and, through my endeavours, I have taken leaps of faith to accomplish some things I never imagined. I want to be one of those faceless lovers of Christ who is willing to step out and touch lives every single day of my life.

I think of heaven and those that are there, rooting for us behind the veil, looking down upon earth as we each run our races. I think of all that will be left standing in the end, one day, is how we Loved. The measure of love I have been given, I want to give it away freely and stand before my maker one day and hear Him say "well done, My daughter. You loved well."

My hope is to hear that.

Psalm 85:10-13 ESV. I thought this
was beautiful as I read these words
today.

*Steadfast love and faithfulness meet;
righteousness and peace kiss each
other. Faithfulness springs up from the
ground, and righteousness looks down
from the sky. Yes, the Lord will give
what is good, and our land will yield
its increase. Righteousness will go
before him and make his footsteps a
way.*

Living a life, even with Jesus by my side,
is not easy. He was perfectly blameless, and
He wants us to co-partner with Him, helping
us one day at a time to do life right with Him.
I am learning it is a lifetime of walking
closely with Him each day, communing and
listening. I desire to be one of the set-apart
ones to be pleasing in His sight. I want to live
in His rest. However, we can be the hands and
feet of love (Jesus Christ) is the meaning of
life in this fallen world. People so desperately
need that meaning in their lives. Let us
become love and make a difference.

I read once that a life lived close to me is
not complicated or cluttered.

The love I am talking about is God's love so different from the world's love or our own emotional interpretation of love. Many things that once troubled me lose their power over me when I rest and give over my concerns to God. The world can be overwhelming, so messy and confusing at times. Living close to Abba requires trust, rest, and intimacy with Him daily.

I choose to renew my mind by reminding myself that God is still in control, and He sees everything that occurs each day everywhere. He said in John 16:33 ESV *I have said these things to you, that in me you may have peace. In the world you will have tribulation. But take heart; I have overcome the world.*

Isn't that a wonderful safety net to know? We can put our trust in Him and have that peace He offers us. He has overcome the world by the cross and the blood that was shed on Calvary by His son Jesus Christ the perfect lamb sacrificed for our sins. He was a man totally human, yet God chose to lay down His life to redeem us and bring each one of us back into restoration with God.

He has overcome the world, and with Him, we can also. I believe it is necessary for us to take His love and give it away to others by being vessels of honour and glory for His sake. We are the hands and feet of love this dying world is waiting to receive.

Hope Nugget: **There is no love without justice & no justice without love.**

TANYA'S STORY

What does it cost to give away the love I am talking about? It costs a listening ear of obedience, your time, and being sensitive to what the Holy Spirit is saying. A few months ago on my social media post, I noticed that a young woman wrote on my friend Trish Wall. She asked Trish, "How do I get one of your friend's books?" I responded with a private message to connect with her. I soon found out she was going through her own dilemma with breast cancer.

We had never met, and I found myself filled with compassion for my unknown friend. I began to pray for her healing and comfort and sent encouraging words to her, hoping God's strength and peace would be the rock she was depending on. She would post her accounts of what she was going through, her oncologist reports, and her fears for the future.

She shared her miracle story of Kelsey and her mom coming into her life to save costs and lend her Kelsey's cold caps to save her hair from falling out from her first round of chemo treatments. I believe Abba was showing Tanya how much He loved her and cared for her by bringing her own angels in the form of love to minister to her as she walked out her own painful cancer journey.

In the middle of May 2019 in my quiet time one morning, she kept coming to my mind, and I had a strong desire that would not leave me to step out and pray for this woman. I thought to myself, "We have never met. Am I crazy?"

Later that day I thought, "I have nothing to lose, and she can say "No" to me, so I messaged her. She responded with, "That would be wonderful. I live in Langley; where do you live? I told her I resided in Abbotsford and I was willing to come out to Langley to meet up with her. Victoria Day on the upcoming long weekend was the day that worked for us both. As I was catching up on email messages that morning and having a quiet time, I noticed it was her birthday that day.

I was delighted this was the day for us to meet and how special that it was on her birthday. I put a couple of items together to bless her on her special day and drove out to the café where we were to meet. She had found a table and was waiting for me. When we recognized each other, I walked over and said, "Hello" and gave her a hug. I was not sure what was going to take place. Her warm reception and grateful smile said it all. She was thankful for the people God was bringing to help her cope and get through this season of her life.

The café was full, with every chair taken, and we were surrounded by the hustle and bustle of noise everywhere. Attentively I listened to her story and felt the emotional pain she was experiencing. I sensed the love of God and His incredible peace around us, like we were being protected from the busyness and lively commotion around us.

When it was time to pray she gave me permission to anoint her with my oil from Israel. The spikenard scent was beautiful, and I put it on her forehead, her hands, and her feet. I took her hands in mine asking the Holy Spirit to come and minister to my sweet friend. It didn't matter to me who was watching or what people thought.

This is what Jesus did regularly. He prayed for, commanded, and healed those who were sick. I was experiencing love in action, just being obedient. He would do the rest. We lingered in the gentleness of His peace as I spoke words of life over her. I was grateful for the healing tears that flowed as I know Abba holds each tear in a bottle for Tanya as He did for me.

When our ministry time together was finished, I told her about a couple of special experiences from my own journey that I thought would bring comfort and hope to her walk. She thanked me and was excited to go out for a birthday dinner that night to one of her favourite restaurants with her family. We hugged good-bye and said we would stay in touch and I know we will. I headed back home, hoping I would not get caught in the long weekend traffic that rainy afternoon. On my way, I thanked God for the opportunity to meet Tanya and to spend a few special hours with her that afternoon, trusting she was in His loving care and He was orchestrating her steps.

Hope Nugget: He has our very best interest at heart; we matter.

HE WILL HEAR

Don't look to the left Don't look to the right
Just look straight ahead just look to the light

Right now, right now.

Cause just when you think that you're quite
alright
Then the pride slips in and you've just lost the
fight
        That's how, yeah that's how.

Chorus:
And when you wait on the Lord
And when you call on His name
He will hear, He will hear.

Keep your eyes on Him Keep the way that's
sure
Keep the pathway clear with a heart that's
pure

Right now Right now.

Let your path be known let your heart be
strong
Let the passion rise, Choosing right from
wrong
That's how Yeah that's how.
          Bert Petkau Dream CD 2011

THE LORD'S PRAYER

One of the most powerful prayers I have come to know is the Lord's Prayer. It is the Word of God written in the Bible in Matthew 6: 9-14 ESV.

When I was a little girl, I remember my mom with her rosary beads reciting the "Our Father" on a regular basis. As a Christ-follower myself, I realize her prayers have availed much in my life including the time in my late teens when her influence led me to Christ. Many of her prayers have made me who I am today, and they have had a huge influence in the destiny and direction of my life.

I remember as a little girl, probably about four years old, when we lived in a little town way up in northern BC because of my father's work. Ocean Falls was the rainiest place ever with snowbanks in the winter that were way bigger than me. It was a pulp and paper mill that employed many people. The town was surrounded by the Pacific Ocean and the only way you could get to this unique place was by boat or plane. Many of the families living there owned boats.

I recall one time when my sister and I were on our boat called "The Cabrini," and we were coming back from somewhere. Out of the small portholes, I could see the waves, tremendously high, swishing water onto the deck of the boat. The storm was vicious, and my father was doing his best to navigate his family back to safety. I remember my mom on her knees with her rosary beads praying out loud, "Our Father, who art in heaven, hallowed be thy name..." I did not understand what was going on then, but I remember I was not afraid. Children with their innocence and natural trusting faith know their parents love them and want to protect them from harm's way. I don't remember what happened after seeing my mom on her knees praying, but I somehow knew we were going to be ok and of course we made it back to shore safely.

I believe God looks at the heart, not at the outward appearance of man. He honoured the faith and consistent prayers of my mom in her own searching way over the years, and she eventually gave her heart to Jesus Christ in her later forties.

It is in a place of intimacy that one of the most effective prayers we can pray is the verse found in the Bible in Matthew 6:10 ESV: *...Your kingdom come, Your will be done on earth as it is in heaven*. I have prayed this verse many times and realize what Jesus was referring to in that line was the Kingdom of God is inside each one of us that believe in Him. When God breathed His life into each one of us at birth, and we accepted His love and forgiveness, each one of us received seeds of the kingdom of God within us. His Spirit is one with our spirits. I find it interesting how Jesus instructs His disciples to also pray this way in Matthew 6:9. ESV Pray then like this: *Our Father in heaven, hallowed be your name.*

When we believe, we carry the kingdom of God in our spirits, and grow it up within. It becomes infectious because the love of God exuded in us to others does spread. Others will become drawn to the love and peace in us. I love the word *infectious*. It also means contagious, spreadable, irresistible, compelling likely to influence others. Is that not what we want? I want to be one of those people who doesn't just have the kingdom of God inside me and does nothing with it. I hope the love of Christ within me exhibits compelling love wherever I go. I have to have the right paradigm embracing the unexpected, becoming a servant, and serving out of delight. I believe changed people change the world, one act of loving service at a time. Jesus at the last supper washed the feet of His disciples, knowing He was going to sacrifice Himself for them and for all of humanity. He became a servant though He was a king. What a powerful thing! He was God yet was a man and became a servant.

My goal is where ever I go, for instance in a grocery store, or at my place of employment, or when I go to the gym and am amongst the community of women I work out with, that they see the presence of God shining through my eyes and sense His peace within me. The power of God has an effect wherever it is displayed. It draws people when it is sacrificial and extravagant. God is so full of mystery, always creating and moving forward, never stale or dull. In order to touch the heart of God, there has to be time spent in intimate relationship with Him every day. He is worth all of our affections and He deserves all the glory.

My view of heaven reflects my view of God. I see heaven as a perfect place where everything is in complete harmony. Revelation 21 1-6 ESV.

Then I saw a new heaven and a new earth, for the first heaven and the first earth had passed away, and the sea was no more. And I saw the holy city, new Jerusalem, coming down out of heaven from God, prepared as a bride adorned for her husband. 3 And I heard a loud voice from the throne saying, "Behold, the dwelling place of God is with man. He will dwell with them, and they will be his people, and God himself will be with them as their God. 4 He will wipe away every tear from their eyes, and death shall be no more, neither shall there be mourning, nor crying, nor pain anymore, for the former things have passed away." 6 And he said to me, "It is done! I am the Alpha and the Omega, the beginning and the end. To the thirsty, I will give from the spring of the water of life without payment.

When I read these verses my heart wells up with anticipation, my eyes get teary with incredible joy and happy tears. One day I again will see those I have loved and love.

Love is the most powerful element that brings hope to others and changes every situation. How God longs to pour His love lavishly on each one of us. He is faithful and true to His word, that although we live in a corrupt and fallen world, we can overcome and He is there to help us and He is true to His promises in our lives. He is a God of order and He will bring the restoration we long for in not only our lives but also those we are contending for through prayer. He is faithful to fulfill His plans and His purposes for our lives when we quietly stay rested in His love.

REFLECTING

As I settle into the routine of my life after walking the Camino Way and reflecting back now upon my travels the past four years, I am transitioning into becoming a woman who is learning to love much and understand a bit of what it is to show compassion, because of the roads I have walked and the challenges I have overcome. Somehow the twists and turns and ups and downs of life have caused me to willingly learn to surrender. I realize I still have holes in my heart. There are scars and bruises yet I know the Holy Spirit is faithful to come alongside me to pour the oil of His Spirit into those places every day as I continue to ask Him to bring healing.

I saw a caption not too long ago that I could relate to.

It said, "Not all storms come to disrupt your life. Some come to clear your path."

I pondered the saying realizing every single one of us is not exempt to facing storms in life. It is embracing them with a peaceful heart and handing the situations over to the care of God. He makes a way to clear a path because we hand over our fears to Him. When we let go and trust He will make a way through the storm. I have read many accounts in the bible of Abraham, Sarah, Rahab, King

David, Queen Esther and the widow in Samuel whom God faithfully provided for. God made a way out for each one of them. We serve a pretty amazing Father who is there in our times of need, and He is faithful to intervene when sometimes in the ninth hour we wonder if He is going to come through!

To focus on God's plan for my life and to stay true to having a relationship with Him daily is my heart's desire. He does clear the path, and He does make a way, when in the natural it seems impossible or unimaginable. I have witnessed His faithfulness over and over again in my own life.

I remember when my children were young, and Bert almost went bankrupt on a construction job we were doing. It was a true miracle how we got through that situation and how God was faithful to provide another job to help us reconcile our dilemma eventually. It was scary at the time, and I learned to surrender as God was faithful to help us throughout that difficult ordeal.

I never dreamed I would lose my husband unexpectedly at such a young age and at a time in our lives where we were happy and enjoying the rhythm we had learned together, doing life well with an appreciation for one another and an excitement for our future together.

Life can hit you out of nowhere, and when it does, if we don't keep our eyes on the storm but rather fixed on Jesus, we realize God has our lives in His hands. He will find us in the difficulties even though answers sometimes seem so far away. I have learned over time that it is how we pick ourselves up and carry on in the journey that really matters.

Sometimes through the discomfort of not knowing what has forged out my life, I have to put my face into the wind and trust God that He is able to work it all out. He does. I have truly seen His loving-kindness make a way when there was no way. He does not leave us or forsake us though at times we wonder. Many times I may not have understood what good could come out of the tragedy and brokenness yet as the years have come and gone and I have stayed true to His faithfulness there is a peace I have learned to rest in and it continues to give me hope. It has become an essential part of my story to encourage others to hope for the same.

It is through facing my fears that I have had the courage to get on an airplane by myself to travel to countries very far away. I never ever thought I would be able to do that. Through my travels over the past four years, I have had wonderful ministry opportunities to come alongside others and to encourage and speak into people's lives. Some of those moments have been in Australia, Brazil, Israel, and Spain. It has opened my eyes to the fact that no matter where we are, we need one another. I also see the importance of recognizing that God can use every opportunity in my life to be His child to bring hope and encouragement to one or many. I was not expecting, three years ago, when doors of ministry just happened to open for me that I would have the privilege to minister to many broken women who were searching for hope and realizing their own need for Jesus in their lives. God is a good Father and one that restores and heals.

I believe in the promise for me of a hope and a future that is bright. Jeremiah 29:11 ESV.

I have seen how many of the decisions I have had to make have been rerouted in a way I never thought possible. God brought the right people into my life to help me deal with impossible situations and for things to be lined up properly personally and in business. It is through His grace and loving-kindness that I have seen every step of every part of my path made clear. 2 Corinthians 2:9 ESV. *What no eye has seen, nor ear heard, nor the heart of man imagined, what God has prepared for those who love him.*

I hang on to this promise with delight looking forward to what He is preparing for me in the next chapter of my life. I urge you to take courage, stay in hope and never give up on being love to others. That is what really matters. What may seem impossible to us is truly possible with God. Never give up.

I have faced the challenge to climb over the Pyrenees mountain range outside Saint-Jean Pied-de-Port on that first day back in September of 2018; 27 km up and 7 km down the mountain and another 3 km walk into the small village of Roncesvalles Spain. On our last day of the trek, I remember in the misty morning cresting over the hill outside Atapuerca village and unexpectedly coming across one of the most stunning wood crosses I have ever seen. In awe of the sunrise appearing early in the morning through the yellow and orange sky, Moira and I stood in amazement with others admiring this unique piece of art. The ambiance was so peaceful. It was one of those rare moments you can't make happen. It was a phenomenon; it was breathtaking. In the stillness of the mist surrounding the morning, an unusual peacefulness filled the air as I dropped my pack to admire, with a sense of wonderment, the mystery and beauty of the cross. I stood there in the quietness of the moment to lift my heart to God and whisper, "Your presence is everywhere." On this last day of my Camino journey in Spain, I thanked Him with a grateful heart for how He has carried me through my ups and my downs and brought some incredible people along my path for me to be encouraged by. If I could have deposited some morsel of His love along the way it had all been a worthwhile adventure.

I look forward to more ventures in my future to distant lands, perhaps hanging out again with Ken & April in Berlin Germany one day, and in the meantime, looking forward to going back to Spain to continue my pilgrimage every step of the way along the Camino de Santiago in May or October of 2020. Now with expectancy I choose to get out of the boat, toss my net on the other side to see what life continues to offer me. I'm willing to take more risks and I marvel at the goodness of God and what he has in store for each one of us. Let Him continue to provoke our hearts.

Buen Camino to each of you "Good Way," as you mark out your own paths embracing the love of God along the way as He directs your steps.

Trust in the Lord with all your heart, and do not lean on your own understanding. In all your ways acknowledge him, and he will make straight your paths. Proverbs 3: 5-6 ESV

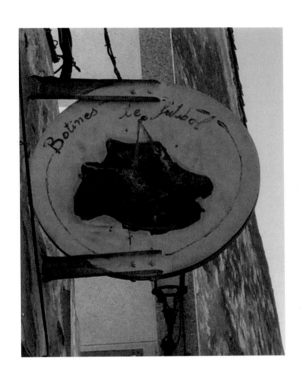

For contact info:
teresapetkau@gmail.com

Made in the USA
Monee, IL
16 February 2020